Jana Milbocker

The Garden Tourist's
FLORIDA

A Guide to 80 Tropical Gardens
in the Sunshine State

Enchanted Gardens

Naples Botanical Garden, Naples

Cover: Florida Botanical Gardens, Largo

Published by Enchanted Gardens
For ordering information please contact
Enchanted Gardens, P.O. Box 6433, Holliston, MA 01746, 508-494-8768, thegardentourist@gmail.com

Cover and interior designed by Jana Milbocker. Photo credits appear on page 203.
Edited by Kathy Brown
Printed in the USA

Publisher's Cataloging-In-Publication Data

(Prepared by The Donohue Group, Inc.)

Names: Milbocker, Jana, author.

Title: The garden tourist's Florida : a guide to 80 tropical gardens in the Sunshine State / Jana Milbocker.

Description: Second edition. | Holliston, MA : Enchanted Gardens, [2024]

Identifiers: ISBN 9780998833538 (paperback)

Subjects: LCSH: Gardens--Florida--Guidebooks. | Gardens--Florida--Pictorial works. | Garden tours--Florida--Guidebooks. | Florida--Guidebooks. | LCGFT: Guidebooks. | Illustrated works.

Classification: LCC SB466.U65 F6 2021 | DDC 635.022/2--dc23

Second Edition

CONTENTS

Sunken Gardens, St. Petersburg

Garden List by Region

Sunken Gardens, St. Petersburg

Harry P. Leu Gardens, Orlando

Marie Selby Botanical Gardens, Sarasota

Introduction

Whether you are an ardent gardener or vacation traveler, Florida offers an abundance of lush gardens to visit. In this book I introduce you to a range of public gardens, from large formal landscapes to off-the-beaten path destinations. While some were designed by renowned landscape architects and others evolved without a formal plan, all of the gardens are the result of their founders' passion for horticulture and the natural world.

In addition to beautiful gardens, many properties offer art, history, architecture, and modern whimsy. Art lovers will enjoy classical sculpture at Albin Polasek's home in Winter Park, the cubist-inspired pieces at the Ann Norton Sculpture Garden in West Palm Beach, European masters at The Ringling in Sarasota, and contemporary sculpture at Peace River Botanical & Sculpture Gardens in Punta Gorda. History and antique buffs will delight in the architecture and collections of the Lightner Museum in St. Augustine, the history of scientific innovation at the Edison and Ford Winter Estates in Fort Myers, and the old-world elegance of Vizcaya in Miami. Some of the gardens are designed for healing, meditation, or quiet contemplation, such as the Garden of Hope and Courage in Naples, Wilmot Botanical Gardens in Gainesville, and Sholom Park in Ocala.

Avid gardeners and plant collectors will be inspired by the horticulture at Naples Botanical Garden, Marie Selby Botanical Gardens in Sarasota, Bok Tower Gardens in Lake Wales, Harry P. Leu Gardens in Orlando, and the Fairchild Tropical Botanic Garden in Miami to name a few. These gardens feature world-renowned plant collections situated in artfully designed landscapes. There are also gardens that preserve bald cypress sloughs, tropical wetlands, hardwood hammocks and other environments indigenous to Florida. McKee Botanical Gardens in Vero Beach and Pinecrest Gardens in Pinecrest preserve some of these special habitats.

Some of the gardens profiled in this book began

as roadside tourist attractions in the early 1900s. Their founders were drawn to the natural beauty of the land. They added native and exotic birds and animals to create vacation destinations for visitors from the North. As tourists drove down Route 1 on the East coast or the Tamiami Trail on the West, they could admire the tropical plants at Sunken Gardens in St. Petersburg, see native birds and mammals at Flamingo Gardens in Davie, feed the flamingos at Sarasota Jungle Gardens, and admire the alligators at the Wonder Gardens in Bonita Springs. In an age of airplane travel and huge amusement parks, these historic attractions hold a special place in Florida's cultural history.

I hope that this guide will help you to discover new destinations in your home state or to plan a vacation in Florida. Happy touring!

Jana Melbocker

Gardening in Florida

TOPOGRAPHY

Geographically, Florida is unlike any other state in the union—a peninsula situated between the Atlantic Ocean, Gulf of Mexico, and Straits of Florida. With a land area of 58,560 square miles, Florida is almost the same size as New England. Although most of the state is low-lying and flat, much of Central and North Florida features rolling hills with elevations ranging from 100 to 250 feet. Close to 50% of the state is covered in forest, and there are more than 30,000 lakes and ponds. Florida has the longest coastline in the contiguous United States, approximately 1,350 miles of beaches, estuaries, seagrass beds, mangrove swamps, and coral reefs.

Throughout most of its history, Florida has been under water. When Pangea began to break apart about 200 million years ago, the landmass that is now Florida submerged beneath the surface of the ocean. As coral, shellfish, and fish skeletons accumulated and disintegrated, a deep layer of limestone, hundreds to thousands of feet thick, settled on the existing bedrock. The great quantities of limestone resulted in an abundance of karst features such as sinkholes, artesian springs, caves, depressions, and limestone outcrops. Today, these sinkholes and springs supply most of the water used by residents. Florida is also home to the second largest freshwater lake in the US, the 700-square-foot Lake Okeechobee.

Florida's limestone foundation is topped with sandy soils that were deposited over millions of years as global sea levels rose and fell. Despite popular conception, Florida is a land of geographic diversity. Northeastern Florida is home to the St. Johns River, flatlands of hardwood forests, and slash pine flatwoods. The Panhandle features low rolling hills and farmland characteristic of the Deep South. Central and South Florida include open forests, grasslands, swamps, lakes, and tropical hardwood forests. South Florida is dominated by the wetlands of the Everglades and Lake Okeechobee.

CLIMATE

Florida is known for its balmy weather, making it a prime tourist destination in the winter months and a haven for retirees. Its climate is tempered by the surrounding ocean, which modulates both winter and summer temperatures and creates humidity. North of Lake Okeechobee, the prevalent climate is humid subtropical, while coastal areas south of the lake have a true tropical climate. Mean high temperatures for late July are low 90°s F, while low temperatures for January range from the low 40°s F in northern Florida to the mid-50°s F in southern Florida. From February to May the weather is sunny and dry, making it a perfect time for visiting gardens.

The seasons in Florida are determined more by rainfall than by temperature, with a wet season from May to October and a dry season from November to April. Florida has the highest average

Region	Climate type	Annual Rainfall	USDA Hardiness Zone
North	Humid subtropical	48-60"	8b (15°F) to 9a (20°F)
Central	Humid subtropical	48-52"	9b (25°F)
Southwest & Southeast	Humid subtropical to tropical rainforest	52-60"	9b (25°F) to 10a (30°F)

precipitation of any state. Afternoon thunderstorms, usually short in duration, are common in most of the state from late spring until early autumn. These thunderstorms are caused by moist air masses from the Gulf of Mexico colliding with those of the Atlantic Ocean. Central Florida has earned the title of "lighting capital of the US" due to the frequency of its lightning strikes.

Hurricanes and tornadoes pose a severe threat to both people and gardens. Florida leads the US in the most tornadoes per square mile, although they are not as intense as in other parts of the country. Hurricane season lasts from the beginning of June to the end of November. Florida is the most hurricane-prone US state, with tropical storms most likely from August to October. It often takes decades for public gardens to recover from the ravages of a tornado or severe hurricane.

GARDEN CALENDAR

Winter in Florida is spring in the rest of the country. Prime tree-planting season occurs from December through February. This is also peak camellia season in the botanical gardens. In February, trees and shrubs burst into bloom. Deciduous fruit trees such as apples, plums, pears, and peaches are rich with flowers, along with azaleas, bougainvilleas, orchid trees, and yellow jasmine. This is May in the North, busy with flower shows, plant sales, and well-stocked nurseries. In March you see dogwoods and viburnums blooming, with cool-season annuals such as geraniums, dianthus, and snapdragons in their prime. Many garden clubs host garden tours this month. April is warm and dry, with gardenias, hibiscus, jasmine, bee balm, daisies, coreopsis, and lantana in bloom. May is the last of the great gardening months with southern magnolias perfuming the air.

Tropical perennials and foliage plants produce their best growth in the heat and humidity of summer. July, August, and September are reminiscent of the tropics, with daily rainstorms, high humidity, and temperatures consistently above 90°F. Bromeliads, birds of paradise, exotic gingers, and vivid hibiscus provide vibrant color in the gardens. Fall begins in October as daytime temperatures drop into the 70°Fs and 80°Fs, and rain showers become less frequent. Cassias, daisies, salvias, and firebushes bloom profusely, and roses come out of their summer hibernation. November and December are great outdoor months, with daytime temperatures in the 70°Fs and 80°Fs, but nighttime dips into the 40°Fs and 50°Fs from Central Florida northward. Citrus trees produce fruit; dogwoods, maples, and sweet gums display colorful foliage; and hollies and beautyberry produce brilliant berries. Cool-season annuals such as pansies, lobelias, violas, and geraniums add punches of color to gardens.

Visiting Tips

GARDEN TOURING PACKING LIST

- ○ GPS/Maps
- ○ Phone/camera
- ○ Small notebook for recording ideas and plant names
- ○ Water and snacks: many places do not have dining options
- ○ Membership cards to gardening organizations. Some gardens participate in reciprocal admission programs.
- ○ Umbrella and rain gear
- ○ Sun glasses, hat and sunscreen
- ○ Sturdy, waterproof walking shoes
- ○ Trunk liner for unexpected plant purchases

NORTH
Suggested Daily Itineraries

Jacksonville Arboretum & Botanical Gardens, Jacksonville (1)
Lunch–Southern Coast Seafood, Jacksonville
Jacksonville Zoo and Gardens, Jacksonville (2)

Cummer Museum of Art & Gardens, Jacksonville (3)
Lunch–Cummer Museum cafe

Flagler College, St. Augustine (4)
Lunch–Harry's Seafood Bar & Grille, St. Augustine
Lightner Museum, St. Augustine (5)

Kanapaha Botanical Gardens, Gainesville (8)
Lunch–Bangkok Square, Gainesville
Wilmot Botanical Gardens, Gainesville (7)
Butterfly Rainforest, Gainesville (6)

Cedar Lakes Woods and Gardens, Williston (9)
Lunch–Shogun Japanese Restaurant, Williston
Sholom Park, Ocala (10)

Dorothy B. Oven Park, Tallahassee (13)
Tallahassee Nursery, Tallahassee
Lunch–Backwoods Crossing, Tallahassee
Alfred B. Maclay Gardens State Park, Tallahassee (12)

Goodwood Museum & Gardens, Tallahassee (15)
Lunch–The Edison, Tallahassee
Cascades Park, Tallahassee (14)

NORTH

Jacksonville Arboretum
& Botanical Gardens

1445 Millcoe Rd., Jacksonville, FL 32225
904-318-4342
jacksonvillearboretum.org

AREA: 120 acres

HOURS: Daily 8–7

ADMISSION: $3

AMENITIES:

EVENTS: Glowing Gardens, Brush with Nature, various educational events

The Jacksonville Arboretum & Botanical Gardens is an urban woodland with three miles of trails that take you through 13 unique ecosystems. The seven individual trails range in difficulty but are all less than a half-mile in length. They will take you above and below a ravine, through xeric hammocks, bottomland forests, across creeks, and around lakes and marshes. Most of the trails are shaded by canopies of red maples, sweet gum, tulip poplars, and several 100-year-old live oaks. Native shrubs form the understory and ferns carpet the forest floor.

The trunks and branches of old live oaks are often covered with the delicate green fronds of resurrection fern. Resurrection fern (*Polypodium polypodiodes*) is an epiphyte that grows on the surface of other plants and trees, most often the live oaks. It is not parasytic—it does not harm the tree at all. It thrives on the moisture and nutrients from the surrounding environment. The fern grows to about one foot in height and spreads widely by slender, creeping rhizomes. Its fronds are deeply cut and leathery. In dry weather the fronds turn brown and curl up, so the fern appears dead. As soon as it rains again, the fronds turn green, and the fern appears to be resurrected.

Throughout the arboretum, you will find almost 600 species of trees, shrubs, and perennials. The Lake Loop Trail circles a two-acre lake surrounded by several garden areas. These gardens focus on all of the different ways that plants are useful to humanity. Some provide construction materials, fibers, latex, oil, resin, dye, plastic, fuel, or other chemicals. The most common are the crops and herbs—plants with edible leaves, shoots, roots, flowers, fruits, or seeds. These include longan, pineapple, goji berry, java plum, and many types of blueberries. A tea garden is planted with *Camellia sinensis*, ginger, hibiscus, holy basil, and tea olive. Medicinal and culinary herbs include hyssop, sassafras, rosemary, mints, cardamom, and black pepper to name a few. A pollinator garden is planted with lantanas, butterfly bushes, salvias, plumbagos, coneflowers, and other plants that provide nectar and pollen for bees, butterflies and birds.

The arboretum has an interesting history. From about 1944 to 1961, strip mines operated in this part of Jacksonville. These mining activities severely impacted the soils and vegetation in parts of the arboretum. In the early 1970s, the City of Jacksonville purchased the property as a passive recreation and open space buffer around an adjacent water treatment plant. The property was largely unused for 30 years, however, and abused by illegal dumping. In 2004 a group of citizens developed a proposal to lease the property for recreational use as an arboretum. The city agreed, and the Jacksonville Arboretum & Botanical Gardens officially opened to the public in November 2008.

Jacksonville Zoo and Gardens

370 Zoo Pkwy., Jacksonville, FL 32218
904-757-4463
jacksonvillezoo.org

AREA: 97 acres

HOURS: Daily 9–5

ADMISSION: $25+

AMENITIES:

EVENTS: ZOOLights, Halloween Spooktacular, special exhibits

For more than a century, Jacksonville Zoo has been a place to view animals from all over the globe. In 2003 the zoo's mission and name changed to reflect a new emphasis on horticulture. The zoo became committed to creating a botanical garden on its property in addition to the plantings that are used in its animal exhibits. Over the last two decades, new themed gardens have been created that add a wonderful new dimension to visiting the zoo, particularly for plant lovers.

Starting at the entry, the Rivers of Color Garden lines the Main Path, adding beauty and interest to this principal thoroughfare. Ornamental trees, shrubs, and perennials add punches of color with their flowers, foliage, berries, and stems. Portions of the garden are changed seasonally to maintain color and interest throughout the year.

Savanna Blooms is the first themed pocket garden that you encounter on the Main Path. This two-acre garden is nestled beneath the Giraffe Overlook and fashioned after a South African oasis. Masses of soft grasses, plumbago, lion's mane, and fine textured acacia leaves are punctuated with palm trees. A serene pool showcases African water lilies and water edge plants. A triangular trellis draped with fragrant flowering vines provides a shady respite, and benches allow you to sit and enjoy a view of the pond.

The Asian Bamboo Garden serves as a gateway to the Asian animal exhibits and includes elements of several Asian cultures. It is entered by the Moon Gate, a traditional Asian gate with a circular entry that symbolizes perfection. The Moon Gate also frames a beautiful view of the Koi Pool within. Rock and water features express the yin/yang principles of Chinese garden design. The Weeping Tree Bridge, which symbolizes a journey, crosses the Koi Pool. Its elliptical shape recalls a rainbow when reflected in the water. The Orchid Pavilion overlooks the Koi Pool and the Yin Yang Terraces. A forest of bamboo flanks the terrace. Bamboo has many symbolic meanings throughout Asia. Its long life makes it a symbol of longevity in China. In Japan, bamboo plantings surround Shinto shrines as sacred barriers against evil. In India, bamboo is a symbol of friendship. In many Asian cultures, bamboo is essential to the creation story: humanity emerges from a bamboo stem.

The Gardens at Trout River Plaza adorn a gathering and event space with a beautiful view of the Trout River. The focal point of the plaza is a fountain with a life-size basking anhinga surrounded by a pebble mosaic that features a menagerie of native animals. Thirteen Grecian-style columns topped with flowering urns and draped in fragrant vines give the garden a classical look. Shade trees, café tables with umbrellas, and a trellis with colorful vines

all create an area for relaxing and special events. Beyond Trout River Plaza, the Riverview Gardens offer tranquil places to sit and enjoy views of birds, insects, and the water. The surrounding gardens are planted with natives that attract and support pollinators and other wildlife.

In addition to the gardens, the animal displays at the Jacksonville Zoo are very innovative in their design and provide a richly immersive experience in landscapes from various regions of the world.

Cummer Museum of Art & Gardens

829 Riverside Ave., Jacksonville, FL 32204
904-356-6857
cummermuseum.org

AREA: 2.5 acres

HOURS: Tues. & Fri. 11–9; Wed., Thurs., Sat. 11–4; Sun. 12–4

ADMISSION: $20

AMENITIES:

EVENTS: Lectures, special exhibits, concerts, classes

The Cummer Museum of Art & Gardens was established in 1958, when art collector, garden enthusiast, and civic leader Ninah M. H. Cummer bequeathed her art collection and riverfront home to create the museum. With 2.5 acres of historic gardens and collections of fine and decorative art, Cummer Museum fulfills its founder's vision of serving "as a center of beauty and culture" in the community.

The gardens were created by one of Jacksonville's prominent families in the early 1900s. Brothers Arthur and Waldo Cummer came from a long line of Michigan lumber barons. They built their homes on either side of their parents on the banks of the St. Johns River. While the brothers led the business, their wives, Ninah and Clara, created the gardens surrounding their homes and became active in the Jacksonville community. Today, three historic garden spaces have been restored to their original glory.

Arthur and Ninah engaged Michigan-based landscape architect Ossian Cole Simonds to create the first plan for their estate in 1903. Simonds' design enhanced the majestic live oaks already on the property with naturalistic sweeps of native trees and shrubs. These plantings provided the backbone for later development. The historic Cummer Oak, with limbs spanning more than 150 feet, still graces the garden today.

In 1910 the Cummers turned to Philadelphia nurserymen Thomas Meehan and Sons for a new design of what is now the English Garden. The garden was redesigned in the Colonial Revival style that was popular during the era and enclosed with an open-brick wall. Rectangular in shape, with beautifully laid brick paths and a central fountain, this garden features some of Ninah's beloved azaleas as well as beds of delphiniums, roses, snapdragons, agapanthus, and other flowers. A striking semicircular cypress-beamed pergola draped with wisteria overlooks the St. Johns River. A beautiful wall fountain, shaded by a wisteria-covered pergola, features intricate castings and inlaid mosaics by Philadelphia artist William Mercer.

In the early 1930s, Waldo and Clara inherited the majority of their parents' estate. They engaged William Lyman Phillips of the Olmsted Brothers firm to incorporate the new property into their existing landscape. Enclosed by high stone walls, the garden features plantings of azaleas, Japanese magnolias, crapemyrtles, hydrangeas, roses, camellias, hollies, palms, and cypresses. A long pergola draped with wisteria provides a shady seating area along one side of the garden.

The jewel in the crown of the Cummer Gardens is the Italian Garden, inspired by Ninah and Arthur's travels through Italy and visits to some of the renowned villa gardens. Ninah worked with landscape designer Ellen Biddle Shipman on the creation of this garden, and it remains one of the few Shipman designs still in existence today. The garden was designed to display Ninah's large collection of Italian marble garden ornaments and hundreds of azaleas. Two long reflecting pools frame the view of the *gloriette*, a curved brick arcade covered with ficus. The gloriette surrounds a circular pool with a tiered marble fountain. Beds of roses, azaleas, perennials, and fastigiate junipers line the reflecting pools and central grass walk.

Since its opening in 1961, the museum's art collection has grown from the core of 60 pieces bequeathed by Ninah Cummer to more than 5,000 works. The Permanent Collection spans from 2100

BC through the 21st century, with paintings, Early Meissen Porcelain, Japanese prints, and five other special collections. A contemporary Sculpture Garden frames the front of the building.

Flagler College

74 King St., St. Augustine, FL 32084
800-304-4208
legacy.flagler.edu

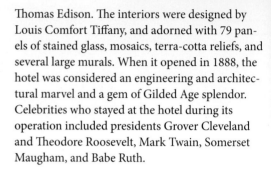

AREA: 47-acre campus

HOURS: Tours by appointment online

ADMISSION: $17

AMENITIES:

Flagler College is considered one of the most beautiful college campuses in America. Located in the historic heart of St. Augustine, the four-year liberal arts college is home to 2,300 students. One of its core values is "thoughtful stewardship," which includes the "preservation of its historical buildings…and natural resources and the celebration of the remarkable heritage of St. Augustine with its vibrant cultures and history."

The historic buildings and grounds of the college were once the opulent Ponce de Leon Hotel, built by oil magnate and railroad tycoon Henry M. Flagler in 1888. Flagler became interested in historic St. Augustine and saw its potential as a winter resort for wealthy Northerners. The hotel was designed in the Spanish Renaissance style. It was the first major project of architectural firm Carrère & Hastings, who later designed the New York Public Library. It was constructed entirely of poured concrete, using the local coquina as aggregate. The hotel was one of the first buildings in the country wired for electricity by Flagler's friend

Thomas Edison. The interiors were designed by Louis Comfort Tiffany, and adorned with 79 panels of stained glass, mosaics, terra-cotta reliefs, and several large murals. When it opened in 1888, the hotel was considered an engineering and architectural marvel and a gem of Gilded Age splendor. Celebrities who stayed at the hotel during its operation included presidents Grover Cleveland and Theodore Roosevelt, Mark Twain, Somerset Maugham, and Babe Ruth.

The former hotel is now Ponce de Leon Hall, the flagship building of the Flagler College campus. The front entrance on King Street is an elegant, semicircular paved plaza with a bronze, life-size statue of Henry Flagler. The plaza brings you to an arcaded loggia with an entry pavilion whose pyramidal roof features an elaborate frieze of putti, peacocks, and seahorses. Tall brick columns with terra-cotta lions' heads flank the gated entrance.

The entry pavilion leads directly into a large courtyard garden. A circular walkway around the perimeter of the courtyard links several entrances to Ponce de Leon Hall, which houses the President's Office and administrative offices. Lush planting beds of palm trees, tropical shrubs, and flowers surround a circular fountain with a tall mosaic column at its center. The fountain is meant to look like the hilt of a sword stuck in the ground. From ground level, you see 12 terra-cotta frogs representing the 12 months around the outer edges of the fountain and four turtles around the base representing the four seasons. When seen from above, you see that the fountain acts as a sundial: the frogs tell the hours, and the turtles tell the minutes. This fountain is not only beautiful but also functional— it was used to aerate the water used in the hotel. The Ponce's beautiful towers once held thousands of gallons of water; today, these towers announce the top of each hour with a different instrumental song.

The west side of Ponce de Leon Hall was originally the "pleasuring ground." Today, this is the West Lawn, a nicely landscaped area with an octagonal brick pavilion and benches for relaxation. Adjacent to this is a small palm garden.

Lightner Museum

75 King St., St. Augustine, FL 32084
904-824-2874
lightnermuseum.org

AREA: Plaza, courtyard, and pocket gardens
HOURS: Daily 9–5
ADMISSION: $19
AMENITIES:
EVENTS: Special exhibits

The Lightner Museum houses a collection of 19th- and early-20th-century furnishings, paintings, decorative arts, and natural history specimens in a gorgeous Gilded Age building that was once the Alcazar Hotel.

The Alcazar was the second grand hotel built by Henry Flagler in 1888 in his quest to create a "Riviera" in St. Augustine. The name Alcazar was Arabic for "royal castle," and the building was designed in a blend of Spanish Renaissance and Moorish styles. The Alcazar was initially conceived as an entertainment annex to its sister, Ponce de Leon Hotel, but it became a grand hotel in its own right. Like the Ponce, it was designed by Carrère and Hastings and built of poured concrete. Its facade was decorated with intricate terra-cotta details and crowned with a pair of iconic twin towers. A formal landscaped plaza separated the two hotels. Today, this large plaza serves as an entry court to the museum, with lawns outlined by sculpted hedges and punctuated with palm trees. The lawns encircle a lovely reflecting pool with a three-tier cast-iron fountain decorated with water birds. A bronze statue dedicated to St. Augustine's founding father, Don Pedro Menendez de Aviles, overlooks the entry.

The Alcazar was designed with three distinct areas: the hotel, the baths, and the casino. The hotel portion at the front of the property framed an interior courtyard lined with shops selling all manner of goods from evening gowns to oriental rugs. It was the spa and recreational facilities that distinguished the Alcazar from other grand hotels. The baths included Turkish (dry heat) and Russian (steam) baths, a cold plunge pool, massage rooms, and a gymnasium. The four-story casino housed the world's largest public indoor swimming pool, an archery range, a bowling alley, and a grand ballroom. In the 1890s the hotel hosted thousands of guests, grand parties, charity events, and celebrations. Due to the Great Depression, the hotel closed in 1930 and remained vacant for 17 years. Today, the hotel portion is home to the St. Augustine Town Hall offices and antique shops. The casino houses the museum and a restaurant on the site of the former swimming pool.

In 1947 Chicago publisher Otto C. Lightner purchased the building and transformed it into a museum to display his collections of fine and decorative art and natural history. You will find everything from player pianos to stuffed birds, model steam engines, cut glass, oil paintings, and marble sculptures, all set within the former Turkish baths and grand ballroom. The museum is entered through the lush, landscaped courtyard, which serves as a popular site for wedding photos. It is planted with tall royal palms, birds of paradise, stands of papyrus and ferns, and bright red caladiums and geraniums. Formal turf beds are outlined with low hedges. The charming stone bridge in the middle of the courtyard is constructed of stones from all around the country and abroad. When work on the bridge began, Lightner published a request for stones in his *Hobbies* magazine. Rocks poured in from readers all over the world: Pompeii, London's Houses of Parliament, Boulder Dam, and various battlegrounds, caves, mansions, and dueling grounds across the US.

Outside the museum, you will find several tiny pocket gardens. The south terrace is being transformed into a recreational area with a community gathering space; an outdoor classroom and art gallery; a community farmers market; and a site for health and wellness programs.

Butterfly Rainforest

3215 Hull Rd., Gainesville, FL 32611
352-846-2000
floridamuseum.ufl.edu

AREA: 6,400 square feet
HOURS: Mon.–Sat. 10–5, Sun. 1–5
ADMISSION: $14
AMENITIES:
EVENTS: Plant sales, many educational events

The Butterfly Rainforest is part of the Florida Museum of Natural History, which is housed in several buildings on the campus of the University of Florida in Gainesville. The rainforest is in McGuire Hall, home to the McGuire Center for Lepidoptera and Biodiversity. This center is the largest in the world devoted to Lepidoptera (moths and butterflies) collections-based research and education. Besides the rainforest and galleries open to the public, the center has more than 31,000 square feet of research labs and 10 million butterfly specimens. The Lepidoptera collection represents most of the world's 20,000 butterfly species and many of the estimated 245,000 moth species. Research scientists and students focus on molecular genetics, microscopy, image analysis, conservation, and breeding of endangered species.

Scientists share their findings with the public through the The Wall of Wings, a massive display that is 21 feet high and 200 feet long. It contains

thousands of scanned images, information panels about butterfly and moth biology, and video screens featuring live footage of butterflies from different parts of the world. Why is Lepidoptera research important? Butterflies and moths are key players in keeping our planet healthy. As pollinators, they transfer pollen from flower to flower in their search for nectar. They themselves are food for other insects, spiders, amphibians, reptiles, birds, and mammals. Because they are sensitive to environmental changes such as pollution and climate change, butterflies are indicators of a healthy environment. Studying butterflies and moths also contributes to our understanding of evolution, genetics, pest control, technology, conservation, and climate change.

The Butterfly Rainforest is a 6,400-square-foot screened enclosure of tropical trees and plants that supports hundreds of living butterflies and moths from all corners of the globe. It's also a place where you can view these amazing insects up close, along with birds, turtles, and fish. A walking trail winds through a lush landscape of palms, orchids, bromeliads, and hundreds of other vibrant flowering plants with ponds and waterfalls adding the soothing sounds of flowing water. You will see butterflies fluttering from plant to plant, basking on leaves, drinking nectar from flowers, and feeding on trays of fresh cut fruit.

Butterflies and moths exhibit several interesting evolutionary traits. Their colors and patterns serve a specific purpose and are essential for the animal's survival. Butterflies are very sensitive to temperatures and can't fly if their body temperature is less than 86°F. Dark colors help butterflies warm up, especially in colder climates. Darker wing scales near the body also help butterflies absorb heat. Males are often much brighter than females to attract a mate. Colors and patterns that blend with the surroundings hide a butterfly from predators. Some, like the bright blue morphos, hide brightly colored wings

and "flash" them to startle predators. Informational panels and skilled interpretive staff are there to answer your questions and provide a personal and engaging experience. And the butterflies are sure to put a smile on your face!

Wilmot Botanical Gardens

2023 Mowry Rd., Gainesville, FL 32610
352-273-5832
wilmotgardens.med.ufl.edu

AREA: 5 acres
HOURS: Daily dawn–dusk
ADMISSION: Free
EVENTS: Two annual plant sales, guided tours available

Wilmot Botanical Gardens is an oasis on the University of Florida campus, situated at the heart of the largest academic health center in the Southeast. The gardens provide a beautiful setting for rest and rejuvenation for patients, staff, faculty, students, and visitors, and have spawned the development of a new therapeutic horticulture program.

Wilmot is named for Royal James "Roy" Wilmot, a UF horticulturist who was both an international authority on camellias and a founding member of the American Camellia Society. When Wilmot died in 1950, friends and colleagues from the US and abroad donated over 300 rare varieties of camellias to the university to create a garden in his memory. As decades passed, the university's medical campus grew around the garden, while hurricanes, pests, and invasive species degraded the once thriving plant collection.

In 2006 Dr. C. Craig Tisher, Dean of the College of Medicine, set out to restore the camellia garden and expand its scope and focus. The plant collections grew to include a Bromeliad Garden and a Japanese Maple Tree Garden. With a gift of 300 camellias and the addition of the Mendenhall Family Camellia Walk, Wilmot became the third garden in Florida to be awarded the American Camellia Trail Gardens designation. Peak camellia bloom is in January.

Today, Wilmot is a botanical garden with a three-pronged mission: "to assist individuals with special needs through a variety of therapeutic horticulture programming, to provide a peaceful refuge for those receiving care at nearby UF Health facilities, and to serve as a living laboratory for medical and other graduate students to learn about these therapeutic techniques." A new Master's degree program in Therapeutic Horticulture was developed to support this mission.

The design of the garden reflects this new mission. New walkways and seating areas were added to make the gardens more accessible to those in wheelchairs and with mobility issues. Eight specialty gardens are located within the five acres. The Hippocratic Garden was created to serve as the site of the College of Medicine's Hippocratic Award ceremony. The sycamore tree in this garden represents the tree under which Hippocrates taught medicine. A 60-meter accessible track was built by the Institute on Aging to examine the effects of exercise on cognitive function in elderly adults. The track encircles a lovely garden and a shady patio with seating. The Chapman Healing Garden was designed to engage all of the senses with plants that exhibit beauty, fragrance, and texture, and a water feature that provides auditory stimulation. The spiral-shaped garden features a central limestone patio with a curved water lily pool, an organic concrete bench, and colorful plantings. A 2,700- square-foot

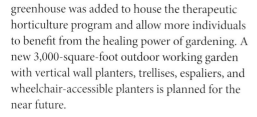

greenhouse was added to house the therapeutic horticulture program and allow more individuals to benefit from the healing power of gardening. A new 3,000-square-foot outdoor working garden with vertical wall planters, trellises, espaliers, and wheelchair-accessible planters is planned for the near future.

Kanapaha Botanical Gardens

4700 SW 58th Dr., Gainesville, FL 32608
352-372-4981
kanapaha.org

AREA: 68 acres
HOURS: Mon.–Wed. 9–5, Fri. 9–5, Sat.–Sun. 9–7 or dusk
ADMISSION: $10 adults
AMENITIES:
EVENTS: Spring Garden Festival, Bamboo Sale, Fall Plant Sale & Orchid Show, and more

Begun with a vision, 33 acres, and a shoe-string budget, Kanapaha Botanical Gardens has grown into one of Florida's largest botanical gardens. Zoologists Don and Jordan Goodman leased the property in 1978. They spent nearly ten years creating the first gardens, building walkways and boardwalks, and constructing gazebos to serve as rain shelters. The site offered a diversity of environments, from mature hardwood forests to rolling meadows, several sinkholes, and magnificent vistas overlooking

the 250-acre Lake Kanapaha. The garden opened to the public in 1987. Its name is derived from the native Timuqua words "palm leaves" and "house," referring to the palm-thatched dwellings of the first human inhabitants of the Lake Kanapaha area.

Since its humble beginnings, the botanical gardens have grown to 68 acres, and the Goodmans' daughter, Alexis Caffrey, now serves as director. Paved walkways wind through 24 themed gardens. While the summer months of June to September offer the most color, the garden is a prime destination year-round.

In addition to gardens devoted to roses, bromeliads, cycads, gingers, ferns, bulbs, aroids, and conifers, you will find a palm hammock and a sinkhole. These sinkholes were formed when the existing limestone bedrock dissolved over the centuries. The Spring Flower Garden is a magnificent woodland garden overlooking the lake, home to hundreds of dogwoods, redbuds, fringe trees, apple trees, red buckeyes, mock oranges, azaleas, and forsythias. These are underplanted with violets, trilliums, and other spring perennials. The Rock Garden is also lovely in spring. It features a central display of cacti and succulents surrounded by a European-style rock garden of flowering plants tucked around stones and boulders. The Vinery features a large collection of ornamental plants with vining habits for both sun and shade. Vine support frames include a gigantic anchor from an early 19th- century English shipping vessel.

Kanapaha's Herb Garden is Florida's largest, with three separate collections, including a medicinal garden and the scented Renaissance knot garden with many culinary herbs.

In the summer the Butterfly and Hummingbird Gardens are in full bloom, with dazzling flowers in shades of red, orange, and yellow that attract pollinators. This is also the best time to see the giant

Victoria water lilies, whose leaves can grow to a diameter of eight feet. Native to the Amazon region, the plants are started from pea-size seeds indoors in February and moved to the garden in May or June. They die once the weather turns cold.

Kanapaha's Bamboo Garden the state's largest public display of bamboos. There is a premier stand of Chinese royal bamboo along with giant timber bamboo, muddy bamboo, blue bamboo, seabreeze bamboo, stripestem bamboo, and variegated Buddha's belly bamboo to name just a few.

Cedar Lakes Woods and Gardens

4990 NE 180th Ave., Williston, FL 32696
352-529-0055
cedarlakeswoodsandgarden.com

AREA: 20 acres

HOURS: Daily 9:30–5. Guided tours available

ADMISSION: $12

AMENITIES:

EVENTS: Spring Festival, Fall Festival, Christmas Lighting

Cedar Lakes Woods and Gardens is one of the most unique landscapes in Florida, located on the site of an abandoned rock quarry. About 50 individual small gardens can be seen on the steep banks and islands of the quarry, among numerous waterfalls, koi ponds, pavilions, and bridges.

The limestone quarry had been used until the 1960s to provide rock for the foundation of Highway 27. When Dr. Raymond Webber discovered it in 1991, it had been abandoned for 30 years and had become a polluted swamp. Dr. Webber, a Williston endodontist, Army reservist, and college lecturer, envisioned the quarry as a perfect fishing

pond. He purchased the land and began cleaning, clearing, and excavating old mining remnants and equipment. The project took on a life of its own, and soon Webber and his team of workers were building islands, concrete walkways, and waterfalls. The islands were then outfitted with gazebos and pavilions, and bridges were built to connect the islands and the walls of the quarry.

Once the infrastructure was created, Webber decided to add greenery, and eventually his interest in plants rivaled his passion for fishing. The protective walls of the quarry create a microclimate perfect for temperate and semi-tropical plants that would not normally grow in north Florida. The quarry walls are lined with concrete and rock planters, filled with hundreds of species of plants and flowers. As you stroll down into the quarry, you will find palms, ferns, azaleas, bougainvilleas, alstroemeria, cycads, gingers, and agapanthus along the winding paths. A red torii gate leads to a Japanese garden planted with Japanese maples, camellias, ferns, and a 142-year-old bonsai. A Japanese red bridge spans a pond with giant koi. Some of the islands are dedicated to certain plant species, such as the cabbage palm island and the bamboo islands. Many of the plants are planted in containers. The quarry can flood during tropical storms (the water level has risen by 10 feet in the past), so the pots allow plants to be moved to higher ground.

The ponds host aquatic plants, including several Victoria water platters, the largest members of the water lily family. The lily pads are up to eight feet in diameter with an upturned rim and a spiny underside that is protects the leaves from browsing fish. Their large white-to-pink blooms only last two days and have a sweet pineapple-like scent. These water platters need water temperatures of 75 degrees year-round, so they are stored indoors for the winter months.

Near the house, you will find an orchard of tanger-ines, figs, persimmons, bananas, loquat, and other fruits, and plantings of roses and azaleas. Webber created a nonprofit and opened the 20-acre gardens to the public in 2014. Adjacent to the gardens is a 64-acre conservation area where you can stroll through a woodland of native oaks, cedars, pines, pecans, hickories, and dogwoods.

Sholom Park

7110 SW 80th Ave., Ocala, FL 34481
352-854-3677
sholompark.org

AREA: 44 acres
HOURS: Daily 8–5
ADMISSION: Free
AMENITIES:
EVENTS: Cultural events, Park After Dark, Spring Strings Concert

Sidney and Ina Colen's vision for a peaceful oasis in Ocala came to fruition in 2004. Sidney had been a prominent developer who moved to Florida from Ohio in 1947. He built numerous senior living communities and cultural and recreational facilities in western and central Florida. The idea for a park was born decades ago while visiting Boston's Public Garden. Sidney found a suitable lot in Ocala with a range of habitats and began collaborating with his son Ken on the design of the project. They named the park after Sidney's grandfather Sholom.

With more than 250 species of plants and trees, Sholom Park is a horticultural destination as well as a place to find inner peace. Two miles of paved walkways wind through 11 unique areas within the park, with numerous benches upon which you may rest as you contemplate the beautiful surroundings. Adjacent to the white alabaster welcome pavilion is

the Formal Garden, lush with palms, ferns, gingers, and flowering shrubs. The Azalea Trail features 700 azaleas that reach a crescendo of bloom in February. The Enchanted Forest is a native hammock with stands of mature oaks, hickories, sweet gums, and long leaf pines. The half-mile Prairie Trail winds around lawns, plantings of grasses and plumbago, and through a butterfly garden. You will also pass a bat house that accommodates 800 insect-devouring bats. The Olive Tree Promenade, with 18 trees planted on each side, is filled with symbolism. The olive branch is a symbol of peace, and the number 18 is a symbol of life in the Jewish faith. The Promenade leads to the Pergebo, a structure that is part pergola and part gazebo, smothered with fragrant confederate jasmine. The Pergebo is made of eight stone-covered columns, aligned so each column is an exact compass direction from the center of the structure. A shady respite, it is the site of weddings and educational programs. The lovely pond is home to giant koi.

The park offers several areas for quiet reflection. One is the Labyrinth, which offers an opportunity for a spiritual or meditative walk along its winding pathway. Labyrinths are ancient garden pathways in an ornamental pattern that encourage a personal experience of reflection for the walker. Twenty-four plaques with inspirational quotes and ideas invite you to reflect on your life and the importance of nature. The second is a new Japanese-style Zen garden with symbolic elements to guide you through a journey of contemplation.

Sidney had a deep desire for world peace. At the very least, he hoped that Sholom Park's peaceful environment would change the world one person at a time. He said, "Let all who enter enjoy nature in the spirit of human enhancement. Let this park be the seed that grows and flowers. Peace is the world's goal."

Hearthstone Gardens

3300 134th Place, Wellborn, FL 32094
386-438-3102
hearthstonegardens.org

AREA: 35 acres
HOURS: Daily dawn–dusk
ADMISSION: Free
AMENITIES:
EVENTS: Workshops, summer camps, April plant sale, October Scarecrow Festival, tours by appointment

Hearthstone Gardens is a dream come true for Judee Mundy, a retired English teacher from Pennsylvania Amish country. More than 20 years ago, Judee began thinking about a creating a tranquil garden that would offer a quiet respite to the public. That dream became a reality when she opened Hearthstone Gardens to visitors in 2018.

Located between the burgeoning towns of Lake City and Live Oak, Hearthstone Gardens is situated on 35 pristine acres of woodlands and fields, nestled between neighboring farms. The site is home to several ponds and is naturally wet, which is both an asset when it comes to irrigation and a challenge when storms flood the area.

Eleven acres were cleared for the formal gardens, which have been designed around various themes. Some are educational, others are tranquil, but all are lovely. The Rose Garden is planted in an "S" pattern with 55 Knock Out rose bushes in shades of red, pink, and white. The roses bloom from spring to fall. The White Patch is a color-themed garden of plants with white flowers or green and white variegated foliage. The color white was selected to evoke peace and serenity. The contrasting Butterfly Garden is planted with colorful perennials such as stokesia, coreopsis, and rudbeckia and annuals such as zinnias and marigolds that are rich in pollen and nectar for butterflies, pollinator insects, and hummingbirds. Other plants serve as hosts for caterpillars.

The large Japanese Garden is one of the newest spaces. It offers a "total change of botanical pace and an injection of a culture known for its simplicity and tranquility." This garden is a North Florida interpretation of a centuries-old traditional strolling garden. Sand paths are shaded by moss-draped live oaks and festooned with white Japanese lanterns. A beautiful red bridge provides views of koi in the pond. Conifers and maples create the perimeter and masses of ornamental grass, bamboo, water-loving irises, and lotus evoke the feel of a Japanese garden.

The Nature Trail winds through the gardens' woodlands and meadows. The trail is made with railroad ties, which gives it a unique and rustic feel. Along the trail, you will find a variety of plants and wildlife, including cypress trees, maples, pines, royal and cinnamon ferns, wildflowers, and birds. There are also several benches along the trail where you can stop and enjoy the scenery.

Judee, still a teacher at heart, offers gardening classes and workshops on a variety of topics and happily shares gardening tips with visitors. A delightful Children's garden has been added with a whimsical gnome house, flower kaleidoscope, story trail, and

other attractions. It is also home to the Learning Center, where budding gardeners can learn about gardens, nature and the environment.

Alfred B. Maclay Gardens State Park

3540 Thomasville Rd., Tallahassee, FL 32309
850-487-4556
floridastateparks.org

AREA: 28 acres

HOURS: Daily 8–sunset; house open during bloom season daily 9–5

ADMISSION: $6 during blooming months (Jan.–Apr.)

AMENITIES:

EVENTS: Annual local garden tour, Camelia Christmas first Friday in Dec., various events

Maclay Gardens has been called a "masterpiece of floral architecture." The gardens were designed and built by Alfred Maclay, who was a wealthy banker and financier from New York. When he visited with his wife, Louise, in 1923, Maclay was impressed by Tallahassee's huge live oaks, pines, American hollies, and blooming dogwoods. He purchased what was then a 1,935-acre quail-hunting plantation and 1,825 acres of adjoining land. He named his estate Killearn after the birthplace of his great-grandfather in Scotland.

From 1923 to1925 the Maclays remodeled the hunting lodge on the property and established the expansive front lawn on the shore of what is now Lake Hall. Work also began on the gardens, which were designed to peak in winter and early spring when the Maclays were in residence. At that time,

hundreds of azaleas, camellias, dogwoods, and native wisterias explode in a crescendo of pinks, purples, reds, and whites. Although self-taught, Alfred was an accomplished landscape designer, and spent hundreds of hours designing the various spaces and creating collections of plants.

Alfred was particularly interested in camellias. He acquired cuttings and plants from gardens all over Tallahassee. He purchased the entire camellia collection of a nursery in Louisiana and bought plants directly from Japanese nurserymen who had settled in the South. He also engaged his friend, camellia nursery owner Breckinridge Gamble, to collect camellias from all over the country. Alfred worked on the gardens until his death in 1944. Today, Maclay Gardens is part of the American Camellia Trail.

At the entrance to the gardens, a wrought iron gate opens upon a long brick walkway that was once the drive to the house. On the upper hillside east of the drive is the Native Plant Garden, with trilliums, golden alexander, viburnums, beautyberry, musclewood, sweet shrubs, silverbell, and red buckeye. It is anchored by a rare Chapman's rhododendron that was found in the wild by friend Jim Fox.

Stately moss-draped live oaks shade the walkway, which is lined with azaleas and mondo grass. A path on the right leads to the Lakeside Pavilion with beautiful views of Lake Hall. Looping past the house, you will find hundreds of camellias growing under the live oak canopy on the hillside. A formal walled garden looks out on a rectangular reflecting pool and Lake Hall in the distance. There are quiet nooks for absorbing nature, a pond edged with daylilies, and a Secret Garden that Alfred used as his quiet workspace. Throughout the garden, mature magnolias, pines, bald cypress, black gum, hickory, and holly trees provide a serene backdrop for the blooming shrubs and perennials.

Dorothy B. Oven Park

3205 Thomasville Rd., Tallahassee, FL 32308
850-891-3915
talgov.com/parks/centers-oven

AREA: 6 acres
HOURS: Daily 7am–11 pm
ADMISSION: Free
AMENITIES:
EVENTS: Holiday light display

Dorothy B. Oven Park includes six acres of walking trails and strolling gardens surrounding a manor house built in 1936. The property has an interesting horticultural history. The land was part of the 1824 Lafayette Land Grant, a gift of 23,000 acres from the US government to General Marquis de Lafayette for his financial support of the American Revolution. The property was later purchased by the Gamble family. Col. Robert Gamble is believed to be the first person to bring a camellia to Tallahassee in 1811. This medium red camellia was later named 'Aunt Jetty' and can still be found in Tallahassee gardens.

Ornamental camellias are native to Asia and were first brought to England aboard a ship of the East India Company in the early 1700s. From England they made their way to the US in the early 1800s. The most important ornamental camellia is *Camellia japonica*, believed to be native to Japan. Depending on the variety, it can be a shrub or small tree, up to 30 or more feet tall. In the wild, it grows as an understory plant on hillsides. *Camellia japonica* has beautiful shiny evergreen leaves and rose-shaped flowers that emerge in winter. Today there are more than 20,000 named hybrids of this plant, with blooms that range in color from white to yellow, pink, salmon, and red. Some flowers are striped or speckled. The flowers sport either a single or a double set of petals. The double flowers vary in style: some resemble anemones, others resemble peonies or roses with prominent anthers. The formal-double shape is unique to camellias.

In the 1920s, Gamble's great-grandson Brecken-ridge established a camellia nursery on the property. He was an avid camellia collector and was said to know the location of every camellia in Tallahassee. He befriended his neighbor Alfred Maclay, who shared a passion for camellias. Gamble traveled throughout the US and abroad in search of new hybrids and shared many of them with Maclay. In return for the camellias, Maclay designed Gamble's house. The property was eventually passed down to Gamble's son Bill Rosa, who worked in the nursery business, and is named after his widow, Dorothy. It was donated to the city by Dorothy's second husband, William Oven, after her death in 1985.

The camellia garden on the grounds of the park was created by the Tallahassee Camellia Society and Garden Club. Beyond the front lawn are plantings of azaleas, which include the native Florida flame azalea (*Rhododendron austrinum*) and the Piedmont azalea (*Rhododendron canescens*). The camellias are at their prime in February and the azaleas from February through mid-March. Hydrangeas, palms, live oaks, and local flora are accented by gazebos, fountains, and benches. The Hillside Gardens behind the manor feature clusters of bamboo and shade-loving plants. The lower garden is a wetland area with streams and a small pond traversed by a long bridge.

Cascades Park

1001 S. Gadsden St., Tallahassee, FL 32301
850-891-3866
talgov.com/parks/parks-cascades.aspx

AREA: 24 acres

HOURS: Daily dawn–dusk

ADMISSION: Free

AMENITIES:

EVENTS: Concerts and many special events

Sometimes referred to as the "Central Park" of Tallahassee, Cascades Park is the crown jewel of the city, a dynamic green space with recreational amenities, a state-of-the-art amphitheater, interactive water fountain, children's play area, historic commemoratives, and miles of multiuse trails. The L-shaped park, with its scenic ponds, waterfalls, mature trees, and lovely plantings, is located just three blocks from the state Capitol, City Hall, and downtown office buildings.

As a city garden, the park was designed to preserve tree groves of century-old live oaks; incorporate native plants that are important to wildlife; and provide green lawns for recreation, trees for shade, and blooming plants for color. You will find allées of sable palms and winding walkways lined with crapemyrtles and nutall oaks. Red Knock Out and 'Veteran's Honor' roses, bright yellow 'Sunshine' ligustrum, sky-blue agapanthus, and orange milkweed provide pops of bright color. A "moon tree," a

sycamore that was grown from a seed that orbited the moon on Apollo XIV in 1971, stands near the intersection of S. Monroe and E. Bloxham streets. The ponds are lined with giant weeping willows, bald cypress and pond cypress, and semi-aquatic plants such as blue flag iris and golden canna lily. Bottlebrush shrubs, milkweed, black-eyed Susans, and other sun-loving flowers provide nectar for butterflies and hummingbirds.

Nearly 2.5 miles of trails offer opportunities for walking, jogging, and biking, with benches and turquoise blue swings for rest and relaxation. Historical features include a Korean War Memorial, Florida's Prime Meridian Marker, and the Smokey Hollow Commemoration—a tribute to an African-American community of the 1900s that once existed on portions of the park. For children, there is the Imagination Fountain, a walk-in fountain with 73 water jets for cooling water play, and the Discovery Zone, a playground built of natural materials featuring a butterfly garden, a log jump, and a sandy beach.

While the park is a wonderful attraction, its transformation is an amazing story. In 2005 this low-lying tract of land was an industrial EPA Superfund site that flooded frequently. The community developed a grand vision for the site, and transformed this forlorn area into a world-class downtown park that serves as a dynamic stormwater management facility. The current park is *designed* to flood. Its large, naturally shaped ponds are connected by meandering streams to hold the water, and six acres of wetlands are filled with plants that treat the water as it flows throughout the site. The native plants and trees throughout the park also create a habitat for wetland creatures. Water from the lower pond is used for irrigation, with fountains and waterfalls designed to provide aeration. This park is an incredible example of beauty, functionality, remediation, and sustainability.

Goodwood Museum & Gardens

1600 Miccosukee Rd., Tallahassee, FL 32308
850-877-4202
goodwoodmuseum.org

AREA: 20 acres
HOURS: Mon.–Fri. 9–5, Sat. 10–2
ADMISSION: $12
AMENITIES:
EVENTS: House tours: Tues.–Fri. 10, 11:30, 1, 2:30; Sat. 10, 11:30, 1 pm; various events

A visit to Goodwood Museum & Gardens is a step back in time to Old Florida charm and splendor. Originally a 1,600-acre cotton plantation, the property features one of the finest antebellum houses in the region, adorned with fine furniture, art, porcelains, textiles, glassware, and mementos. The mansion is surrounded by 16 historic out-buildings and centuries-old live oaks and gardens.

Goodwood's history began with a passion for botany. Hardy Croom purchased the 2,400 acres upon which the Goodwood Plantation was built in 1834. A cultured man and lawyer by profession, Croom was a naturalist with a passion for horticulture. He was a member of the Academy of Natural Sciences of Philadelphia as well as the New York Lyceum of Natural History, and a friend of John James Audubon. Croom visited Florida several times and considered it a "Garden of Eden," filled with new and unusual plants. His most famous find is the torreya tree (*Torreya taxifolia*), a member of the yew family, which he named for his friend, botanist Dr. John Torrey. Torreya's native range was restricted to a 20-mile area along the slopes and ravines of the Apalachicola River. In turn, Torrey named a woodland wildflower Croom had discovered *Croomia pauciflora*. Both plants remain rare and endangered today.

Croom never lived on his plantation—he and his family perished at sea on their voyage to Florida. His brother Bryan inherited the land and built the brick and stucco manor home. He expanded the estate, creating one of the largest plantations in upper-middle Florida. Goodwood went through many owners in its 180-year history, and the gardens did not become an important feature until after the Civil War. During the Croom plantation era, formal gardens were rare and very small. The emphasis was on a beautiful dirt yard around the house that was swept every evening. This kept bugs and vermin away and revealed any footprints of intruders creeping up to the windows and doors, which stayed open at night to cool the house.

As you tour the grounds today, they feel old and relaxed, and each area is a little different in style based on its creator. In the late 1800s, Elizabeth Harris Arrowsmith installed the charming Gazing Globe Garden and planted magnolias and fruit trees. In the early 1900s, Fanny Tiers renovated both the house and gardens for winter entertaining. She added Colonial Revival architectural features, such as the pergola-framed pool and terraces, and planted new exotic and tropical species. In 1925 Senator William Hodges and his wife, Margaret, brought a love of gardening to the estate. They built the greenhouse, created the formal rose garden, planted camellias and other flowering shrubs, and added thousands of bulbs. After the senator died and Margaret remarried, her second husband set up a foundation in her name to ensure that Goodwood would outlast them both. When the foundation inherited the property in the 1990s, it decided to focus on heirloom plants that existed in the region before 1930. Senator Hodges had carefully documented "the arrangement of the plantings" in 1926, which serves as a valuable blueprint for garden restoration.

Chapman Botanical Gardens

177 5th St., Apalachicola, FL 32302
850-653-1210
floridastateparks.org/learn/chapman-botanical-gardens

AREA: 1 acre
HOURS: Daily 8–dusk
ADMISSION: Free

Chapman Botanical Gardens is a hidden gem in Apalachicola. The gardens are named after Dr. Alvin Chapman, a respected 19th-century plant hunter and botanist. Dr. Chapman was a physician and a "Union Man" from Massachusetts with a degree from Amherst College. At a time when the classification of plants was confined to the Northeast, Chapman began collecting plants in Territorial Florida that were unknown to his northern colleagues. His collection area was described as "terra incognita" in the *Botanical Gazette*.

Chapman settled in Apalachicola in 1847. As a plant explorer, Chapman befriended and explored the region with Hardy Croom, the original owner of Goodwood in Tallahassee, and botanist John Torrey. During his 50 years of research, Chapman roamed far and wide through the South. His ex-

plorations took him from the swamps of Florida to the mountains of the Appalachians, giving him the opportunity to discover new species of plants while documenting countless others. His forays into the pine woods and swamps of Florida lasted well into his 80s. One of his specimens had a label stating "Collected by A. W. Chapman, walking thirteen miles for this plant, in his eighty-third year." Chapman discovered an amazing variety of new plants, including the extremely rare Chapman's Rhododendron, the custard apple (*Annona squamosa*), the wild Florida azalea (*Rhododendron canescens*), the large-flowered skullcap (*Scutellaria montana*), the spreading yellow foxglove (*Aureolaria patula*), and many others. With assistance from Harvard University's president Asa Gray, he published his seminal work *Flora of the Southern United States* in 1860. The book was the first comprehensive description of plants outside the Northeast and is still considered an important reference volume on plants of the South.

The Chapman Botanical Gardens were first conceived in the 1980s by city planner John Myers, who encouraged Apalachicola to create them to honor the legacy of their famous botanist. Walking the half-mile loop that winds throughout the gardens takes you through both cultivated and naturalistic spaces.

As you enter through the pavilion, you will find a beautifully composed garden of cacti and succulents to your left. Further on the right, the butterfly garden is an excellent place to simply relax while an array of native and migratory butterflies flutter around you. Brightly colored flowers attract nectar-seeking pollinators. The path continues through other habitats, with several seating areas to rest, including a gazebo.

On one end of the gardens, the paved walkway leads to an elevated boardwalk that takes you over a small marsh area. This section was created to give

(L-R) Chapman's Rhododendron, custard apple, large-flowered skullcap

visitors an idea of what the area looked like before settlers arrived. Wetlands like these brought both life and death to early Florida settlers. The marshes are natural filters that clean the water as it flows through them, allowing the shrimp and oyster beds of Apalachicola Bay to thrive. They also serve as breeding places for mosquitoes, which caused the malaria and yellow fever epidemics that ravaged the city in the 1800s.

Eden Gardens State Park

181 Eden Gardens Rd., Santa Rosa Beach, FL 32459
850-267-8320
floridastateparks.org/parks-and-trails/eden-gardens-state-park

AREA: 3 acres of gardens, 163 acres total

HOURS: Daily 8 am–sunset; guided house tours Thurs.–Mon., hourly 10–3

ADMISSION: $4 per vehicle, $4 house tour

AMENITIES: 🌳 👥 🏛️

EVENTS: Camellia Festival, Christmas Candlelight Tour

Entering Eden Gardens State Park is reminiscent of visiting a plantation in the Old South. The elegant white house with columns and a wraparound porch is surrounded by moss-draped live oaks and ornamental gardens. During guided tours of the estate, park rangers share the history of the home and its owners, the timber industry, and life as it was in Old Florida.

The house was built in 1897 by William Henry Wesley, a prominent lumberman. According to local legend, Wesley designed the house based on a Southern plantation that offered him food and shelter during his journey home at the end of the Civil War. During the late 1800s, lumber production was a major industry in the region. The Wesley Lumber Company was one of the largest lumber operations in the area, and the Wesley estate was the company's busy headquarters. In addition to the mansion, a sawmill, commissary, and 20 company-owned houses for the employees occupied the site. Lumber was cut at the saw mill, loaded onto barges, and shipped downriver. Wesley descendants lived in the home until 1953, and then it remained uninhabited for 10 years.

When New York heiress Lois Genevieve Maxon discovered the abandoned estate in 1963, the old house and its oak-shaded grounds had fallen on hard times. Maxon saw the property's innate beauty and potential, and she spent the next five years painstakingly renovating and enlarging the home. She created a showplace with family antiques and heirlooms, including a collection of Louis XVI furnishings that is the second largest in the country. Maxon also developed the ornamental gardens around the property. Due to failing health, Maxon donated Eden Gardens to the state of Florida in 1968.

Touring the grounds, you will find groves of camellias and azaleas in the shade of the old live oaks. They bloom from October to mid-May, peaking in early March. A large rectangular reflecting pool creates a dramatic focal point in the lawn. Nearby is the "wedding tree," a stately live oak that figures prominently in many wedding photos. A formal rose garden is accented with brick walkways and statuary. A shady hidden garden is home to a pond with a whimsical fountain of children fishing. From the hidden garden, a walking trail winds around the perimeter and leads to a charming picnic area overlooking Tucker Bayou. There are several benches placed strategically throughout for rest and contemplation.

CENTRAL
Suggested Daily Itineraries

Washington Oaks Gardens State Park, Palm Coast (1)
Lunch–Alfies, Ormond Beach
Ormond Memorial Gardens, Ormond Beach (2)
The Casements/Rockefeller Gardens, Ormond Beach (3)

Kraft Azalea Gardens, Winter Park (11)
Mead Botanical Garden, Winter Park (8)
Central Park Rose Garden, Winter Park (10)
Lunch–Bosphorous Turkish Cuisine, Winter Park
Albin Polasek Museum & Sculpture Gardens, Winter Park (9)

Dickson Azalea Park, Orlando (14)
Lunch–Farm & Haus, Orlando
Harry P. Leu Gardens, Orlando (13)

Walt Disney World Resort, Orlando (15)
Lunch–Walt Disney World Resort

Bok Tower Gardens, Lake Wales (17)
Lunch–Bok Tower Gardens Cafe

Hollis Garden, Lakeland (18)
Lunch–Fish City Grill, Lakeland
Bonnet Springs Park (19)

Florida Botanical Gardens, Largo (22)
Lunch–Roosterfish Grill, Largo

The Dalí Museum, St. Petersburg (25)
Lunch–The Dalí Museum Cafe
Sunken Gardens, St. Petersburg (24)
Gizella Kopsick Arboretum, St. Petersburg (23)

14   **21**   **24**

CENTRAL

Washington Oaks Gardens State Park

6400 N. Ocean Shore Dr., Palm Coast, FL 32137
386-446-6783
washingtonoaks.org

AREA: 20 acres of gardens, 425 acres total

HOURS: Daily 8–sunset

ADMISSION: $5 per vehicle

AMENITIES:

EVENTS: Annual Mother's Day Weekend Plant Sale, Annual Garden Party

Nestled between the Atlantic Ocean and the Matanzas River, Washington Oaks Gardens State Park preserves 425 acres of beautiful coastal scenery. The park offers trails for hiking and biking, opportunities for birding, fishing, and beachcombing, and 20 acres of formal gardens.

The gardens and buildings are the legacy of Louise and Owen Young from New York who purchased the property in 1936 as a winter retirement home. Owen was a lawyer, diplomat, counsel to five presidents, chairman of the board of General Electric, and founder of RCA. Louise was a designer and businesswoman with lingerie and fine linen shops and interests in weaving and pottery. She used her artistic talent to design the house and gardens. Despite their wealth, the Owens built a modest home that overlooked the river and a separate building for Owen to conduct his business. They gradually purchased beachfront property across the road.

Surrounded by coastal scrub and tidal marshes, the gardens are located in a shady hammock of tower-

ing live oaks, hickories, and magnolias. Southern live oaks (*Quercus virginiana*) are majestic trees that have become emblems of the South. As their Latin name suggests, they are native from Virginia south to Florida and west to Texas and Oklahoma. Unlike most oak trees which are deciduous, southern live oaks are nearly evergreen. They replace their leaves over a short period of several weeks in the spring. When given enough room to grow, their sweeping limbs plunge toward the ground before shooting upward, creating a distinctive form. They are fast-growing trees, reaching heights of 50 feet with crowns that can reach diameters of 150 feet. The oldest live oaks in the country are estimated to be more than a thousand years old.

The gardens at Washington Oaks consist of formal plantings within a jungle setting, with elements of English and Asian garden design. The magnificent live oaks offer shade as you stroll down mondo grass-edged pathways through themed gardens and around lovely ponds. Gazebos and well-placed benches provide lovely views. Louise was a talented gardener and filled the garden with her favor-

ites—camellias, azaleas, orchids, and citrus, all of which can be seen in the garden today. A formal rectangular rose garden is an oasis of color and perfume. Rose bushes tower to heights of eight feet and include the deep crimson 'Don Juan,' coral 'Tropicana,' carmine 'Kentucky Derby,' pink 'Sweet Surrender,' yellow 'Sun Flare,' and apricot 'Medallion.'

The sandy soil and subtropical climate at Washington Oaks are ideal for growing citrus. The first orange groves here were established by John Moultrie, Lt. Governor of British Florida in the 1700s. In the 1800s subsequent owners Joseph Hernandez and George L. Washington grew oranges and shipped them upriver by sailboat to St. Augustine. The Youngs expanded the diversity of citrus at Washington Oaks with plantings of sweet oranges, grapefruits, lemons, limes, and tangerines. At one time, Louise attempted to establish a citrus business. Owen loved the orange groves, and occasionally the wealthy industrialist set up crates by the road and sold fruit to tourists.

Ormond Memorial Gardens

78 E. Granada Blvd., Ormond Beach, FL 32176
386-676-3347
ormondartmuseum.org/art-garden/the-gardens

AREA: 2.5 acres

HOURS: Gardens: daily sunrise–sunset;
museum: Mon.–Fri. 10–4, Sat. 12–4

ADMISSION: Free

AMENITIES:

Ormond Memorial Gardens is a lush oasis surrounding the Ormond Memorial Art Museum. Although the gardens are located in the heart of the city, the combination of manicured landscaping and naturally wild gardens gives a feeling of being in a tropical rain forest.

The museum was founded in 1946 to house a collection of 56 symbolic paintings donated by celebrated artist and illustrator Malcolm Fraser. The gardens commemorate the service of American veterans. A monument with an American flag honors soldiers who served in World War I, and a bronze plaque inside the museum lists Ormond Beach residents who served and died in World War II. There are also sculptures in the Memorial Gardens dedicated to American soldiers who fought in

the Korean and Vietnam wars. In addition to the Fraser collection, the museum features Florida and national artists, an annual student exhibition, and programs for veterans.

The gardens were designed in the 1940s by Chicago landscape architect Henry Stockman, who trained in Belgium. They were built on a former sand dune and evolved around the land's contours. Natural depressions were made into ponds, and the small hill, which is the highest elevation in Ormond Beach, became the site of the waterfall. Winding paths provide the illusion of a much larger garden. Stockman utilized both native and exotic plants in a rich tapestry of palms, bromeliads, hibiscus, begonias, ferns, and cycads. The gardens have been tended by garden artisan Janett Van Wicklen Taylor for more than three decades.

The Peacock Fountain graces the pool at the museum's south entrance. The peacock sculpture was created by Malcolm Fraser's wife, Mary Aldrich

Fraser, an artist in her own right. You will see slider turtles at the base of the foundtain. They may appear to be part of the sculpture, but they are alive! Be sure to look through the flower kaleidoscope next to the fountain.

On the right is the impressive waterfall surrounded by colorful foliage plants. Five ponds in total add the sounds of gurgling water throughout the garden, and provide homes for turtles, frogs, and fish. They are filled with aquatic plants such as water hyacinths, which supply food and shade for the wildlife, and clean the water. The three natural ponds are ringed with marginal bog plants such as papyrus, bananas, and ginger lilies. Benches throughout the garden provide quiet areas for contemplation. A painted labyrinth inside the gazebo invites you to "follow the path walking slowly towards the center, release concerns and let go. Stand quietly in the center, seeking a peaceful space within. Retracing your steps, be open to receive new insights, peace, and healing."

The Casements/Rockefeller Gardens

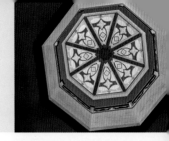

25 Riverside Dr., Ormond Beach, FL 32176
386-676-3216
thecasements.net

AREA: 9 acres
HOURS: Mon.–Fri. 8–5, Sat. 8–12
ADMISSION: Free
AMENITIES:
EVENTS: Gallery exhibits, Art in the Park, movies

The Casements is a historic property with beautiful views of the Halifax River. Built in 1913, it was purchased in 1918 by John D. Rockefeller and served as his winter home for the last 20 years of his life.

When Rockefeller purchased The Casements, so named for its charming casement windows, he enlarged the house but left it unadorned. His retirement years in Ormond Beach were quiet and peaceful, spent golfing, riding in his chauffeured

car, and attending weekly concerts in the Ormond Hotel that was across the street. "Neighbor John," as he preferred to be called, enjoyed taking part in community activities. He would sing with the villagers and hand out his customary dimes to children and adults. He loved watching the automobile races on the beaches of Ormond and Daytona and entertained friends Thomas Edison, Henry Ford, and Harvey Firestone. Each year he hosted a huge Christmas party for neighbors and friends, a tradition carried on to this day by The Casements Guild.

When Rockefeller purchased the property, it consisted of nine acres that stretched east from the river to the present day Halifax Drive. A private trail and right-of-way led to the Atlantic Ocean. Rockefeller worked with a Swedish landscape designer to develop the gardens in a formal style with expansive views of the river. The gardens included citrus trees, a grand promenade, streams with small bridges, and beds of seasonal flowers.

After Rockefeller's death, The Casements was sold, and subsequently served as a college for young women, a retirement home, and an apartment hotel. When it was left vacant in the 1970s, vandals and fire extensively damaged the home. It deteriorated until it was placed on the National Register of Historic Places in 1973. The property was then purchased and restored by the City of Ormond Beach. Today, the mansion is a community center offering classes, workshops, and special events.

Extensive renovations were done in 2009 to create an attractive five-acre community park called Rockefeller Gardens. The highlight of the park is the restored promenade along the river that is widely used for strolling and enjoying the views. Across from the mansion, an outdoor stage is the site of many weddings. A small pond features a fountain with a sculpture of a silver king tarpon, *Megalops Atlanticus*. The grounds are adorned with azaleas, roses, and masses of flowers.

Dunlawton Sugar Mills Gardens

950 Old Sugar Mill Rd., Port Orange, FL 32129
info@dunlawtonsugarmillgardens.org
dunlawtonsugarmillgardens.org

AREA: 10 acres

HOURS: Daily 8–5

ADMISSION: Free

AMENITIES:

EVENTS: Plant sales

Dunlawton Sugar Mill Gardens has a colorful history that includes land deals, Seminole Indian Wars, the Civil War, whales, and dinosaurs. Before Florida gained its statehood in 1845, its land was divided and sold as large land grants by Spain. Dunlawton Sugar Mill Gardens is located on a 995-acre land grant purchased in 1804 by Patrick Dean, who grew indigo, sugar cane, rice, and cotton on the property. Later owners produced sugar and molasses. The plantation was burned down during the Seminole Indian Wars in 1835 and 1856. During the Civil War, it served as the headquarters for the St. John Rangers, and its kettles were used for the production of ammunition. A giant live oak named the Confederate Oak still stands near the sugar mill where it sheltered camping soldiers. After the war, settlers used the sugar mill kettles to distill seawater into salt to cure their meat, and to render oil from two whales that beached themselves in Port Orange.

In the 1870s the plantation was purchased by Charles Dougherty, Florida's first US Congressman, and eventually divided and sold off in smaller lots. In the late 1940s, the property was leased to Dr. Perry Sperber, who created an amusement park called Bongoland. The park featured a small zoo with bears, macaws, parrots, a chimp named Bongo, a tiny Seminole Indian village, and four cement dinosaurs. The venture was not a success, but the dinosaurs still grace the gardens today, along with a giant cement ground sloth added in recent years. The property's last owner, J. Saxton Lloyd, willed it to Volusia County in 1963, and it became the site of

the Botanical Gardens of Volusia in 1985.

The Botanical Gardens organization has created about 20 different garden areas. Some gardens focus on educating local gardeners about the plants that do well in this part of Florida. Others create a beautiful setting for visitors to enjoy while they explore the mill ruins. Collections of azaleas, bulbs, native plants, ivies, cycads, bromeliads, and tropicals provide color throughout. You will find an Asian garden, a butterfly garden, a gnome garden, a human sundial, a grotto, and a secluded nature's chapel. The mill ruins feature original sugar mill equipment such as a sugar cane crusher that was once powered by a horse. Interpretive signs recount the history of the mill and of the pioneers who braved the harsh New World conditions in an effort to make a living refining sugar cane.

The gardens have become a focus for the Port Orange community. You will find Eagle Scout projects, such as a lovely bridge, gracing the landscape. Volunteer gardeners meet twice weekly to keep the gardens looking their best.

Discovery Gardens

1951 Woodlea Rd., Tavares, FL 32778
352-343-4101
sfyl.ifas.ufl.edu

AREA: 3.5 acres
HOURS: Mon.–Fri. 9–4, third Sat. 9–4
ADMISSION: Free
AMENITIES:
EVENTS: Landscape & Garden Fair, classes, guided tours

Discovery Gardens calls itself "a feast for the senses and an outdoor classroom" and it truly is both of these. The 3.5- acre public garden is located at the University of Florida/Institute of Food and Agricultural Sciences (UF/IFAS) Lake County Extension Office in Tavares. It showcases 24 themed landscapes suitable for Central Florida.

Just inside the front entrance is a Little Free Library filled with gardening books to share, a wonderful idea for any public garden. The Tropical Shade

Garden is the first stop and features lady palms, Chinese fan palms, huge philodendrons, and birds of paradise. These are underplanted with a variety of cycads and hundreds of bromeliads. As one Master Gardener explained to me, the bromeliads with spikes along their leaves generally prefer the sunnier locations while those with smooth leaf edges thrive in the shade.

Beyond the Tropical Gardens is the Children's Garden with a Butterfly Garden, a Maze, a Backyard Habitat with birdhouses and gnomes, a Five Senses Garden planted in raised concrete containers and the Orchid House.

You can stroll along a zigzag wooden boardwalk through the Palm Garden and arrive in an area that showcases garden styles from around the world. Each garden has a pergola or gazebo with seating styled to fit into its cultural theme. The English-style Cottage Garden features plantings of roses, carnations, blackberry lily, yarrow, shrimp plant, and other flowers that thrive in Florida. The Southwest Garden welcomes you with large cacti and plantings of agaves, kalanchoes, crown of thorns, and yuccas. A teal pergola and whitewashed walls are reminiscent of New Mexico. The Asian-style Meditation Garden is surrounded with a bamboo fence and displays contorted mulberry, a cloud-pruned Yaupon holly, various bamboos, weeping bottlebrush, ground-hugging junipers, and the architectural elkhorn fern, all accented with Japanese lanterns and other accessories. Across the walkway, you enter through a mandevilla-covered arch into the Mediterranean courtyard garden, with a formal layout, a central tiered fountain, boxwood hedges, and olive trees in the four corners.

True to its educational mission, Discovery Gardens demonstrates water-wise gardening, native plantings, rain gardening, and an interesting comparison of groundcovers and various turf grasses for homeowners. The Kitchen/Herb garden is set up in

elevated wooden beds, perfect for aging or special needs gardeners. There are gardens dedicated to all kinds of edibles from tree fruit to berries, grapes, and vegetables. A Hydroponics Garden features an astounding bounty of vegetables grown in stacked hydroponic containers.

Wildflower and nectar gardens teach visitors about the importance of pollinator plants. Discovery Gardens hosts numerous educational programs for homeowners, and Master Gardeners are always on hand to answer questions.

Central Florida Zoo & Botanical Gardens

3755 W. Seminole Blvd., Sanford, FL 32771
407-323-4450
centralfloridazoo.org

AREA: 26 acres of exhibits

HOURS: Daily 9–4

ADMISSION: $23.95

AMENITIES: 👫 🏪 🍼

EVENTS: Animal encounters and tours

The Central Florida Zoo began in 1923 with the gift of a a rhesus monkey to the Sanford Elks Club. Soon a female monkey, bulldog, skunk, possum, raccoon, and squirrel were added to the collection, which was transferred to the Sanford Fire Department. By the 1940s the zoo boasted new facilities with a "Monkey Island" and lions. With the donation of 106 acres by Seminole County, the zoo finally moved to its current home on the shore of Lake Monroe and construction of the current campus began. Today, it is home to 400 animals, an insect zoo, a reptile house, and educational exhibits and shows.

Due to their climate, all Florida zoos have the look of lush tropical jungles. But in the early 2000s, the zoo began to focus on expanding its botanical exhibits and achieved botanical garden status in 2007. The property already possessed a collection of native trees, palms, and bamboos. Collections of bromeliads and ferns were added. The animal habitats were planted with "browse plants" that the animals can eat to enrich their diets or use for foraging and nesting purposes.

New display gardens were built to educate visitors about invasive plants and Florida-friendly plants such as aroids, bromeliads, and cycads. The Butterfly Garden provides host plants for caterpillars and nectar-rich flowers for native butterflies. The Health and Wellness Garden showcases herbs for medicinal and culinary uses. The Spines, Thorns, and Prickles Garden displays agaves, colorful kalanchoes, snake plants, crown of thorns, and a variety of cacti. An educational sign in this garden

explains how these "porcupines of the plant kingdom" developed sharp defense mechanisms to avoid being eaten. Crown of thorns (*Euphorbia milii*) is a semi-succulent that is popular in hot and dry gardens throughout Florida. It was named after the Greek physician Euphorbus and Baron Milius, who introduced the species to Europe in 1821. Native to Madagascar, the plant gets its common name from the legend that the thorny crown worn by Jesus at his crucifixion was made from this plant. There are an amazing number of hybrids and cultivars, with flowers in shades of red to yellow, pink, salmon, and creamy white.

Jim Houser Azalea Gardens

701 Old Horatio Ave., Maitland, FL 32751
407-539-6200
maitland.recdesk.com

AREA: 1.5 acres

HOURS: Daily dawn–dusk

ADMISSION: Free

The Jim Houser Azalea Gardens is a lovely pocket garden of towering live oaks underplanted with colorful azaleas and tropical plants. Winding pathways invite you to stroll through the lush plantings and benches beckon for relaxation.

The park was acquired by the city in 1977. It was christened the Jim Houser Azalea Gardens in 1993 to commemorate Mayor Houser who had been instrumental in making the lovely azalea gardens a reality. Jim Houser was a beloved public servant with a long list of contributions to the city dating back to 1960. He served as mayor of Maitland from 1978 through 1984 and on the City Council for several terms. A brilliant MIT-educated mathematician, Houser was an aeronautical engineer with Martin Marietta Aerospace and moved to Central Florida during the pivotal years of the space industry. Upon his retirement, he dedicated his life to improving his community.

The gardens began with a dense canopy of oak trees that provided a perfect microclimate for azaleas, which require protection from the strong Florida sun. The azaleas bloom in shades of magenta, red, apricot, pale pink, and white from early February through March.

The park was rebuilt and rededicated in Houser's honor in 2015 with many attractive plantings, benches, and walkways. African lilies (agapanthus), variegated shell ginger, bromeliads, and 'Gold Mound' duranta were planted to add interest to the garden with their varying forms, flowers, and colorful foliage.

An important improvement was the installation of permeable walkways made of a rubberized material that comes from recycled automobile tires. This creates a new use for materials that would normally end up in a landfill and provides a cushioned walking surface for visitors. The permeable surface also allows rainwater to percolate directly into the ground below to replenish the aquifer.

Mead Botanical Garden

1300 S. Denning Dr., Winter Park, FL 32789
407-622-6323
meadgarden.org

AREA: 48 acres

HOURS: Daily 8–dusk

ADMISSION: Free

AMENITIES:

EVENTS: Camellia Show, Backyard Biodiversity Day, concerts, Great Duck Derby

Tucked away on the southern border of Winter Park, Mead Botanical Garden features a variety of natural ecosystems, a boardwalk through 12 acres of forested wetlands, a creek, and display and demonstration gardens of flowers and unusual plants. It is a great spot for bird watching, community gatherings, and cultural events.

The botanical garden was founded to honor Theodore L. Mead, an eminent naturalist, entomologist and horticulturist. As an entomologist, Mead discovered more than 20 new species of butterflies in North America. In fact, it was a butterfly collecting trip that first brought him to Florida in 1869. He saw the potential of the area for cultivating semi-tropical plants, and eventually settled in Oviedo near Lake Charm. Mead became a close friend and colleague of Henry Nehrling (see Nehrling Gardens) and collaborated with him on horticultural research and hybridizing. Both men shared a passion for caladiums and amaryllis, and introduced many significant new varieties.

Mead was also famous for his work on crinums, daylilies and bromeliads. In the 1920s, he was the first American to hybridize bromeliads, a family of plants which includes the ornamental foliage plants as well as tillandias (air plants) and ananas (pineapple.) Today, there are more than 2,500 species and several thousand bromeliad hybrids grown in the world, and they are one of the most popular ornamental plants in Florida landscapes.

Mead's most significant contributions were in the field of orchid hybridizing which was extremely challenging during that time. Mead applied his

scientific background and research skills both to creating new crosses and also to developing laboratory conditions that made this work possible on a larger scale. His work was instrumental in creating a viable orchid industry. When he passed away in 1936, his two friends and colleagues, Jack Connery and Rollins College professor Dr. Edwin Grover, founded the botanical garden in his memory.

Today Mead Botanical Garden is devoted to educating the public about the importance and diversity of plants. Its cultivated gardens and natural biological communities display interesting plants from around the world, as well as species from Florida's native wetlands and uplands. These can be seen along the trails and in the Native Plant Demonstration Gardens, which feature plantings of beautyberry, saw palmetto, Southern magnolia, Southern red cedar, and many others. Two butterfly gardens provide habitat for caterpillars and nectar and pollen for pollinators. The Legacy Garden showcases a collection of tropicals with colorful foliage and flowers. The Camellia Garden is exquisite in February when hundreds of flowers bloom in shades of pink, red, and white.

In Mead's parking lot, you will also find a William Bartram Trail marker dedicated by National Garden Clubs. It commemorate the famous naturalist's plant hunting expedition in the southern states in 1773-77 and his discovery of much of Florida's native flora and fauna.

Albin Polasek Museum & Sculpture Gardens

633 Osceola Ave., Winter Park, FL 32789
407-647-6294
polasek.org

AREA: 3.5 acres
HOURS: Tues.–Sat. 10–4, Sun. 1–4
ADMISSION: $12
AMENITIES:
EVENTS: Special exhibits, concerts

The tranquil gardens at the Albin Polasek Museum are an integral part of the story of the internationally renowned sculptor. Many of the sculptures were created here by Albin Polasek after he survived a debilitating stroke that left him paralyzed on the left side of his body. Yet he continued to paint, draw, sculpt clay, and, with assistance, carve stone. These gardens are not only beautiful to behold but part of Polasek's inspirational legacy.

In 1950 Polasek, then aged 70, retired to Winter Park after a successful 30-year career as a sculptor of public and private commissions and head of the Sculpture Department at the Art Institute of Chicago. He had been born in 1879 in Moravia (a region of the Czech Republic) and apprenticed with a woodcarver in Vienna before immigrating to the

United States in 1901. After four years of carving ecclesiastical sculptures for churches throughout the Midwest, Polasek began formal training at the Pennsylvania Academy of the Fine Arts and later at the American Academy of Art in Rome. Large public commissions in Europe and the US brought him success and an international reputation.

When he came to Winter Park, Polasek designed his home, studio, and gardens with Old World charm. The stucco home, with its tiled roofs, gentle rounded facade, and warm ochre color, is reminiscent of Moravian cottages. The interior is filled with paintings, sculptures, a private chapel, and mementos from family, friends, and travels abroad.

Polasek designed the gardens himself as a beautiful setting for his artwork. More than 50 sculptures are carefully situated with groupings of tropical plants or with a panorama of Lake Osceola as their background. Their themes are taken from history, mythology, and folklore. Many are earlier works whose originals grace churches and museums all over the world. In front of the house you will find one of Polasek's most famous pieces, *Man Carving His Own Destiny*, an homage to his personal struggle to establish himself in the world. Originally conceived in

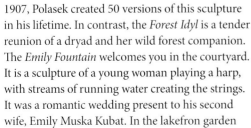

1907, Polasek created 50 versions of this sculpture in his lifetime. In contrast, the *Forest Idyl* is a tender reunion of a dryad and her wild forest companion. The *Emily Fountain* welcomes you in the courtyard. It is a sculpture of a young woman playing a harp, with streams of running water creating the strings. It was a romantic wedding present to his second wife, Emily Muska Kubat. In the lakefron garden

behind the house you will find *The Victorious Christ* and the *Stations of the Cross*, which are mounted on a curved wall covered with ivy. *Unfettered*, a beautiful bronze of a woman reaching for the sky, is Polasek's vision of a woman breaking through the clouds of ignorance and superstition into the full light of freedom. The mysterious *Water Goblin*, based on a Czech folktale, perches at the edge of a pond in a dark grotto. The collection of sculptures— some figurative, some deeply religious, or mythological, tell the story of Polasek's life.

Central Park Rose Garden

251 S. Park Ave., Winter Park, FL 32789
407-599-3334
cityofwinterpark.org

AREA: .5 acre garden, 11-acre park
HOURS: Daily dawn–dusk
ADMISSION: Free
EVENTS: Sidewalk Art Festival, 4th of July celebration

Located in Winter Park's busy downtown shopping district, Central Park is the heart of the city and the site of numerous events and activities throughout the year.

In 1904 Charles Hosmer Morse, a Chicago industrialist and philanthropist, purchased vast tracts of land in Winter Park. He envisioned Winter Park as a thriving, culturally rich city, and began development projects that would enhance the town for its residents and visitors. Morse gave Winter Park its first town hall and donated land and buildings to a wide variety of civic organizations. In 1906 he deeded the land that is now Central Park to the town, with the stipulation that the parcel could not be developed and would remain open to the public. Today, Central Park is the hub of a charming historic downtown, with fountains, benches, and tree-lined walkways.

The Rose Garden at the far south side of Central Park holds 154 roses in eight flower beds. The rose varieties include 'Belinda's Dream,' 'Beverly,' 'Love and Peace,' 'Moonstone,' 'St. Patrick,' 'Grenada' 'Angel Face,' and 'Christian Dior.'

Framing the garden on one end is a brick-columned pergola draped with a petrea vine (*Petrea volubilis*). Also called queen's wreath, petrea blossoms with billowing clouds of cascading purple star-shaped flowers. The enormous flower clusters can reach up to a foot in length and completely cover this handsome plant in spring. Blooms will then appear on and off in summer with another burst of flowers in the fall. The fast-growing woody vine is similar to wisteria but not as invasive.

The focal point of the Rose Garden is a pool with a bronze peacock fountain. Peacocks have a special history in Winter Park. Hugh McKean, former president of Rollins College, and his wife Jeannette, granddaughter of Charles Morse and founder of the Morse Museum, brought the first peacock to Winter Park in 1950. They moved to the Windsong estate, which Jeanette inherited, and made it open to the public. The peacock population soared into the hundreds in the 1960s. When most of the estate was sold off for development, the peacocks dwindled to a flock of 18 in what is now the Genius Drive Nature Preserve. Peacocks often roam through surrounding neighborhoods, where residents enjoy watching and feeding them. The peacock has become the official symbol for Winter Park and is featured on the city seal.

The seven-foot bronze peacock fountain in Central Park was designed by Lloyd Leblanc and installed in 2014. The idea for the fountain came from 15-year-old John Michael Thomas, who raised $50,000 for its purchase and installation as his Eagle Scout project. The fountain was dedicated in memory of his childhood friend Elizabeth Buckley who died of a brain tumor at the age of 13 and was a big fan of peacocks.

Kraft Azalea Gardens

1365 Alabama Dr., Winter Park, FL 32789
407-599-3334
cityofwinterpark.org

AREA: 5 acres
HOURS: Daily 8 am–dusk
ADMISSION: Free

Winter Park's hidden gem is Kraft Azalea Gardens, located in a lovely neighborhood on Alabama Drive along the shoreline of Lake Maitland. With five acres of landscaped paths, azaleas, towering trees dripping with moss, and water views, it is a beautiful and secluded oasis.

The park bears monuments to two men who were instrumental in its creation: George Kraft, a successful businessman, and Leonard J. Hackney. a former Supreme Court judge. Both men retired to Winter Park in the 1920s. At that time, the park along Lake Maitland's south shore had been created but not developed. The two men worked together to transform the park into a beautiful lush garden. Kraft and his landscape gardener propagated azaleas via cuttings from his own garden. As the shrubs matured, they were transplanted to the park. Kraft's wife, Maud, served as chairwoman in the Winter Park Garden Club, which took an active role in maintaining the park.

Hackney served as chair of the Azalea Garden Committee, and supervised the transformation of the park into a showplace. Orlando nurseryman Martin J. Daetwyler was hired to develop plans for the park's layout, which included walking trails bordered by masses of azaleas under towering live oaks and Spanish moss canopies. Daetwyler took over much of the planting of the park, and in 1934 the city became responsible for its maintenance. Upon Kraft's death, his family set up a trust fund for the park's maintenance, and the park was renamed Kraft Azalea Gardens.

Florida gardens generally feature Southern Indica azaleas, which are hybrids of Asian species. Some of the most popular cultivars include 'George Lindley Tabor,' a variety that produces countless soft pink flowers and grows to 10 feet tall and 8 feet wide; 'Brilliant' with carmine red flowers; 'Formosa' with deep rose-purple flowers; and 'Mrs. G. G. Gerbing' with white flowers.

The most striking feature in the park is the exedra, a curved structure with Greek columns and a bench at its base that overlooks the lake. The monument is 18 feet wide and 14 feet tall. It was donated in 1970 by Kenneth and Elizabeth Kraft to honor George and Maud. The word *exedra* comes from the Greek "ex" (out) and "hedra" (seat). Exedras can be architectural niches for sculptures. Most often they are used in gardens to provide enclosed seating or to commemorate an event or individual. The intimate rounded shape encourages conversation. The Kraft exedra overlooks the lake, providing beautiful views and a lovely backdrop for photos. Its inscription reads: "Pause friend. Let beauty refresh the spirit."

Kraft Azalea Gardens is a peaceful setting, ideal for photography, picnics, weddings, watching sunsets, and observing birds. The property is a rookery for great egrets and barred owls as well as many varieties of waterfowl. During my visit, I observed an anhinga drying its wings on the shore and nine great egrets nesting in a towering live oak by the road.

"Pause friend.
Let beauty refresh the spirit."

Walt Disney World Resort

Orlando, FL
disneyworld.disney.go.com

AREA: Parks range from 142 to 500 acres

HOURS: Various, see website

ADMISSION: Various, see website

AMENITIES: 👫 🏠 ✕ 🚼

EVENTS: Various, see website

Beyond its rides, characters and attractions, Walt Disney World is one of the largest gardens in the world with more than 40 square miles of plant displays. Walt Disney alway considered landscaping as an integral element of the park. When planning Disneyland in California, he traveled to Europe several times and brought home notebooks filled with inspiration and gardening techniques. He was particularly impressed with Copenhagen's Tivoli Gardens, and wanted his own parks to overflow with beautiful flowers and color. As a result, floriculture and horticulture have been big features at each of the Disney parks.

To build Walt Disney World, Walt acquired 27,000 acres of mostly swampland and scrub forest in Orlando. The site needed massive improvement before the resort could be built. Thousands of workers moved 8 million cubic yards of soil and built 55 miles of levees and canals to create a blank slate for the design of the landscape.

Each park's landscape design and accompanying plants serve many purposes and have many distinctive styles. Some, such as Victoria Gardens at Canada in Epcot's World Showcase, are attractions in their own rights. Most of the gardens function as beautiful set designs, enhancing the theme of each park with their selection of plants, color, layout and accessories. Each park has a style that is carefully orchestrated–whether it is the turn-of-the-century, small-town America style of Main Street USA in The Magic Kingdom, or the relaxed vibe and tropical, lush plantings of Typhoon Lagoon. Much of Animal Kingdom evokes the landscapes Asia, with plants and cultural elements from India, Tibet, Thailand and many other countries.

Nowhere are the landscapes more varied than at Epcot, where each of the pavilions in the World Showcase features plants and designs that reflect its country of origin. Whenever possible, plants native to each country are used, whether it is olive trees in Italy, or Japanese maples in Japan. The landscape design and architectural features truly make you feel like you have stepped into another country—whether it is the Shakespeare parterre with a bust of the poet in Britain; or a pond encircled with bamboo and panda topiaries in China; or Future World's sweeping geometric beds of brightly colored flowers that underscore the contemporary

style of Spaceship Earth.

Many of the plantings have practical purposes as well. Tall trees provide a shady respite from the sun, and groupings of plants screen unwanted views and distractions. Islands of plantings direct traffic throughout the park, and provide privacy and cozy enclosures for dining and relaxation.

When you look at Disney World's statistics, the size of the operation becomes evident. Between 700 and 800 horticultural professionals tend 3.5 million bedding plants, herbs and vegetables, and care for the 175,000 trees, 4 million shrubs, 13,000 rose bushes, and 800 hanging baskets. They create more than 200 pieces of topiary, from traditionally sculpted hedges to fanciful three-dimensional Disney characters. The plants come from about 50 countries and every continent except Antarctica.

The work of the horticultural team goes far beyond the creation of the beautiful landscapes. The team also grows food for the guests in The Land Pavilion, testing new techniques and growing a whopping 30 tons of fruits, vegetables and herbs that are served in Disney World restaurants and donated to local food banks. They also select and tend plants for the animals at Disney's Animal Kingdom, and make sure that the horticulture in these locations is edible, safe and palatable for the animals living there. With 2,000 acres of grass that needs to be pristine at all times, there are staff members dedicated to mowing and fertilizing these extensive lawns. Disney World horticulturists also partner with The University of Florida to explore new techniques in horticulture and conservation for responsible stewardship of the landscape.

An excellent time for visit Disney World is during the annual Epcot International Flower and Garden Festival, which typically runs from March through May. The three-month spectacle features additional gardens and topiaries, outdoor kitchens with special foods, and talks and activities centered around home gardening. Epcot also features the Living with the Land attraction, a gentle boat tour through multimedia agricultural displays and the four working greenhouse of The Land Pavilion. You can also take the Behind the Seeds Tour here to discover the Disney's innovative gardening techniques.

UCF Meditation Garden

Honors College, 12778 Aquarius Agora Dr., Orlando, FL 32816
407-823-2076
ucf.edu

AREA: 1 acre
HOURS: Daily dawn–dusk
ADMISSION: Free

The Burnett Honors College is considered the jewel of the University of Central Florida, providing its 1,700 students with unique learning and research opportunities. Its building was completed in 2002 and features classrooms, computer labs, offices, lecture halls, a study lounge, and a beautiful Meditation Garden. The Meditation Garden was designed as a special place for students and faculty to contemplate, relax, study, and commune with one another in a tranquil setting.

The garden is sheltered from the campus with a waist-high brick wall and a screen of golden bamboo, which creates a gentle rustling background. As you enter the garden, you will find a pond with a small waterfall and several huge koi. The pond is bordered by bromeliads and other tropicals.

A curving walkway leads through the garden to the building entrance. Tables with umbrellas, long curved benches, and a lounge area with soft furnishings provide spaces for outdoor lunches, informal meetings, and socializing. Pink and yellow trumpet trees (*Handroanthus impetiginosa* and *Tabebuia aurea*) bestow filtered shade and gorgeous flowers from January to March. Trumpet trees are fast growing and can reach a spread of 25 to 35 feet. Their leaves are reminiscent of the native red buckeye, with five palmately divided leaflets. They are deciduous for a short time in late winter. When their leaves drop, the trees are covered in masses of trumpet-shaped flowers.

A dry creek bed runs along the brick wall and is home to many varieties of bromeliads and gingers. The bed terminates at a circular brick patio with a curved metal bench surrounding a central mule palm. The palm resembles a giant umbrella and provides dappled shade and the gentle crackling sound of its fronds. Magenta and purple cordylines, golden variegated shell gingers, and pink and red bromeliad blooms add bright splashes of color.

Harry P. Leu Gardens

1920 N. Forest Ave., Orlando, FL 32803
407-246-2620
leugardens.org

AREA: 50 acres

HOURS: Daily 9–5

ADMISSION: $15

AMENITIES:

EVENTS: Special events, exhibits, classes and camps

Harry P. Leu Gardens is the premier botanical garden in the Orlando area, with significant plant collections and themed gardens for the plant collector and home gardener. The gardens and historic home were deeded to the City of Orlando in 1961 by Orlando native Harry P. Leu and his wife, Mary Jane. Harry owned one of the largest industrial supply companies in Florida. The Leus purchased the 50-acre property on Lake Rowena in 1936 and restored the historic house, which dated back to the mid-1800s. Over the course of 25 years, they transformed the landscape into a local showplace featuring camellias, roses, azaleas, and exotic plants that they brought home from their travels abroad.

Today, Leu Gardens is a botanical oasis in the middle of the city, with 40 different plant collections. The Camellia Collection ranks among the largest in the United States. Camellias were Harry's favorite plants, and he created a major collection of *Camellia japonica* and *Camellia sasanqua* varities. More

than 1,700 plants and 250 cultivars are displayed throughout the gardens. They thrive in the shade of mature oaks and grace the garden with their gorgeous flowers from mid-October through March.

Mary Jane was passionate about roses, and she created a small rose garden in 1944 on the banks of the lake. Today, Leu Gardens features one of the largest formal rose gardens in Florida, with 650 roses in beds surrounding an elegant fountain. The 25 varieties include old garden roses and modern hybrids. All are suited for Central Florida growing conditions.

The Tropical Stream Garden transports you into a tropical rainforest with a gurgling stream. The towering palms, banyans, bananas, and flowering trees are densely underplanted with colorful birds-of-paradise, bromeliads, calatheas, crotons, gingers, heliconias, and ti plants. Leu Gardens' aroid collection is also found here, with caladiums, monsteras, philodendrons, anthuriums, dieffenbachias, and other exotics.

The Idea Garden is an excellent resource for home gardeners, with ten residentially scaled theme gardens showcasing noteworthy plants, materials, and growing techniques. There is a Fragrance Garden, Ornamental Grass Garden, Subtropical Fruit Garden, Wildflower Garden, Shade Garden, Perennial

Garden, and an Urban Patio Garden. The Bird Garden displays plants that attract birds with their fruits and berries. The Bog Garden demonstrates plants that tolerate wet locations, areas where water can stand for several hours to a couple of days at a time following a heavy rainfall. The Enabling Garden illustrates ways in which gardening can be adapted for those with special needs. Raised beds provide accessibility for visitors in wheelchairs and those with visual impairments.

Other special features include Camphor Row, an allée of giant camphor trees (*Cinnamomum camphora*) that were planted in 1900 and lined the Leus' driveway. The trees are native to Asia and are very aromatic. They are the source of camphor oil and other essential oils widely used in medicines and insect repellents. The White Garden displays shrubs and flowers with white blooms or green and white variegated foliage. A charming vegetable, herb, and butterfly garden area features pollinator plants, culinary and medicinal herbs, and seasonal vegetables suitable for Central Florida.

Dickson Azalea Park

100 Rosearden Dr., Orlando, FL 32803

407-246-2121

orlando.gov/Parks-the-Environment/Directory/Dickson-Azalea-Park

AREA: 3.6 acres

HOURS: Daily sunrise–sunset

ADMISSION: Free

Dickson Azalea Park is a green gem located in a neighborhood of quiet streets and attractive homes. With its sunken location, winding paths, lush plantings, singing birds, and the gentle sound of water flowing in Fern Creek, the park is an oasis in the busy city of Orlando.

Dickson Azalea Park began as a watering hole for cattle herders in Florida's early history. It became a park in 1924 when State Senator Walter Rose donated the land to the City of Orlando for public enjoyment. In 1926 the Washington Street Bridge, one of the park's major highlights, was built. The

white bridge illustrates a unique South Florida style. During the Great Depression, civic organizations kept the park beautiful through the Works Progress Administration.

The current park was designed in 1935 with the aid of botanist Mulford B. Foster who preserved native plants and added berrying trees and shrubs to encourage a bird sanctuary. Local groups including the Orlando Garden Club, First Methodist Church, employees of Dickson & Ives department store, and the *Sentinel Star* newspaper adopted plots within the park to beautify. Dickson Azalea Park was dedicated on February 21, 1937, honoring Henry Hill Dickson, a pioneer Orlando businessman and advocate of the city's beautification. In 1941 the park became the official home to Orlando's Garden Center and the seat of the Orlando Garden Club, who held their meetings there for about 10 years. During World War II the club donated the garden center to the Red Cross Defense Unit for use as its headquarters. Although there have been many changes in the park over the years, efforts have always been made to preserve its historic background.

Today, you will find winding trails, terraces, stairs, and numerous bridges crisscrossing Fern Creek, amongst lush plantings of palms, camellias, and native trees. Hundreds of azaleas bloom from mid-February through March in shades of deep pink, carmine red, and apricot. Although most of the azaleas are evergreen, they produce so many flowers simultaneously that you can barely see the foliage. Florida gardens generally feature Southern Indica hybrids, with their tolerance of strong sun, heat, and humidity, and hardiness in Zones 6 to 9. These hybrids grow six to eight feet tall and wide and sport large funnel-shaped flowers. The flowers are favored by hummingbirds. Dickson Azalea Park is adjacent to Mayor Carl T. Langford Park, which offers picnicking spaces and playgrounds for children.

Nehrling Gardens

2267 Hempel Ave., Gotha, FL 34734
407-445-9977
nehrlinggardens.org

AREA: 6 acres

HOURS: Tues.–Wed. 10–2; first & second Saturdays 9–3

ADMISSION: $5 donation

AMENITIES:

EVENTS: Private tours by appointment, plant sales

Nehrling Gardens is an important historic garden that greatly affected the horticulture industry in Florida. The former home and trial garden of renowned botanist Dr. Henry Nehrling, today it is a community resource and education center focused on historic preservation, horticultural education and environmental conservation.

A German American, Dr. Nehrling was born in Wisconsin in 1853, and became an accomplished ornithologist who wrote about birds in German and in English. He became interested in tropical plants, and in 1885 purchased 65 acres in the newly settled German-American town of Gotha, where he could pursue his new passion. Twenty five acres of prime land became one of Florida's earliest experimental botanical gardens. In 1902 Dr. Nehrling moved his family to Gotha and the 1880s Florida wood frame vernacular style home that you see today.

In the early 1900s Dr. Nehrling's Palm Cottage Gardens became one of Florida's first USDA horticultural experimental stations where Dr. Nehrling

tested more than 3000 new and rare plants. His detailed descriptions and observations of tropical and subtropical plants, written for a variety of scholarly journals and magazines, established him as an expert in the field. More than 300 of the plants that he tested became important ornamental plants in Florida, including caladiums, palms, bamboos, magnolias, amaryllis, Indian Hawthorne, and crinum lilies.

Dr. Nehrling's interest in caladium dated back to 1893, when he visited the Chicago Columbian Exposition and was smitten by these Brazilian natives. Caladiums are tropical perennials with colorful leaves in shades of green, white, pink, rose and red. The leaves may be heart-shaped or strappy with ruffled edges, contrasting margins, and mottled, veined, and striped patterns. Dr. Nehrling bred and grew them in massive quantities, perhaps having as many as a quarter million plants representing a couple thousand varieties.

The garden became a popular destination for botanists, tourists, nature lovers, and new Florida settlers. Dr. Nehrling was very generous with his plants and knowledge. Many prominent people of the era, such as Theodore Roosevelt, Thomas Edison, Theodore Mead, and Dr. David Fairchild, marveled at the garden and celebrated Nehrling's extraordinary contributions to horticulture. Today the Henry Nehrling Society is working to save this important piece of Florida's pioneer history and share it with the public.

Bok Tower Gardens

1151 Tower Blvd., Lake Wales, FL 33853
863-676-1408
boktowergardens.org

AREA: 70 acres
HOURS: Daily 8–6; see website for El Retiro hours
ADMISSION: $20, $10 additional for El Retiro
AMENITIES:
EVENTS: Carillon concerts at 1 pm and 3 pm daily, walking tours at noon and 2 pm

Designed by renowned landscape architect Frederick Law Olmsted Jr., Bok Tower Gardens is a romantic garden sanctuary with lush seasonal plantings, informal woodlands, gorgeous vistas, and a world-famous carillon tower.

In 1923 Olmsted was commissioned by Edward W. Bok to transform a sandhill in Central Florida into "a spot of beauty second to none in the country." Bok was a magazine editor, a Pulitzer-Prize winning author, and a philanthropist. Born in the Netherlands, he immigrated to the US at the age of six and grew up in poverty in Brooklyn, New York. Working his way up in the publishing industry, Bok served as editor of *The Ladies Home Journal* for more than 30 years and increased its circulation to more than one million subscribers. During his tenure, the magazine focused on domestic architecture, social causes, and progressive ideas, and it

included building plans for affordable houses for the American middle class.

Bok and his wife, Cynthia, wintered near Lake Wales Ridge and loved the beauty of the area. They purchased 25 acres on the ridge's highest hill to protect the land from being developed and to create a sanctuary for both people and wildlife. Olmsted and his team worked on the garden for five years, planting a mix of tropical and native plants that would support migrating birds and local wildlife. Olmsted's plan included the planting of 1,000 mature live oaks, 10,000 azaleas, and hundreds of magnolias, palms, gordonias, camellias, hollies, and blueberries.

In 1925 Bok decided to replace the property's water tower with a stone water and bell tower that was both utilitarian and beautiful. The resulting 205-foot-tall neo-Gothic Singing Tower was sited at the highest elevation on the property. A team of architects and artisans created a masterpiece of pink marble and coquina decorated with sculpture, metalwork, and mosaics with spiritual and natural themes. The sculptures and grillwork depict cranes, herons, eagles, seahorses, jellyfish, fin fish, pelicans, flamingos, geese, swans, foxes, storks, tortoises, hares, baboons, Adam and Eve, and the serpent. The Great Brass Door features 30 scenes from the Book of Genesis. A 60-bell carillon occupies the

bell tower, and a wide moat filled with koi surrounds the base. A reflecting pool north of the tower captures its entire image.

The gardens have grown and evolved in the decades since the Boks' ownership, but their emphasis has remained on natural habitats and plant conservation. A 23,000- square-foot Pollinator Garden attracts birds, bees, butterflies, and other insects. The Endangered Plant Garden educates visitors about plants facing extinction in their native habitats. The Wild Garden displays four diverse native environments—pine savanna, oak hammock, wetland prairie, and bog—and a 170-foot-long boardwalk overlooking the Wildlife Pond. The Window by the Pond allows visitors to watch birds, reptiles, butterflies, and other animals in their natural habitat. A sign proclaims, "This is nature's show, not ours. No scheduled performances."

The nature theme is also evident in the whimsical Hammock Hollow children's garden that invites discovery-based learning about the natural world. Entered through a miniature moon gate, the garden incorporates fountains, spray jets, and misters; a stage for little performers; limestone ledges, boardwalks, and stumps for climbing and hopping;

fairy houses for imagining; sand pits for excavating; and acoustic instruments for creating music. Giant acorn sculptures and stone mosaic woodpeckers, gopher tortoises, frogs, butterflies, and an immense indigo snake adorn the playful spaces. Hammock Hollow is a wonderful immersion in the natural world for the young and the young at heart.

Bok Tower Gardens also includes El Retiro, a 20-room Mediterranean-style mansion surrounded by lush gardens. The estate was built in the 1930s as a winter home for Charles Austin Buck, vice president of Bethlehem Steel. Buck was enamored with nature, gardens, Latin architecture and lifestyle, and named his home El Retiro, which means "retreat" in Spanish. He hired landscape architect William Lyman Phillips of the Olmsted Brothers firm and architect Charles Wait to collaborate on the project. The garden was actually designed first, and the house was positioned later for a seamless flow between indoors and outdoors. The 12,900-square-foot villa features a barrel-tile roof, thick walls, large porches, heavy carved wooden doors, intricate wrought iron, and Spanish tile.

A tour of the property begins with a walk through a grove of orange trees, camellias, and bromeliads that leads to the walled East Terrace. The terrace is shaded by large trees hung with Spanish moss and palms underplanted with mondo grass. This is a formal Mediterranean-style garden with rectangular beds, boxwood hedging, hand-painted

tiles adorning the steps and curved bench, and a lovely Spanish frog fountain. A path leads guests to a small stone grotto at the front of the house. Kumquats, camellias, roses, begonias, firecracker plants (*Russelia*), and agaves fill the garden with color and dramatic forms. Buck requested a modest entry door so that the emphasis would remain on the entry garden.

To continue the flow of indoor and outdoor spaces, Phillips designed a formal, rectangular terrace garden outside the dining room porch. The garden leads to an octagonal moon gate with a decorative screen, which overlooks a small fountain. Behind the tall wall enclosing the parking area is a charming pocket garden with a moss-draped crapemyrtle and perennial beds enclosed with yew hedges.

The gardens behind the house were designed in a naturalistic style. Sloping down from the house, the rolling West Lawn provides beautiful views from the house, with a scenic pond to reflect sunsets. Several large flower beds are planted with annuals and a desert garden features cacti, agaves, sedums, and Mexican feather grass. Buck also requested

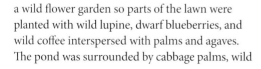

a wild flower garden so parts of the lawn were planted with wild lupine, dwarf blueberries, and wild coffee interspersed with palms and agaves. The pond was surrounded by cabbage palms, wild coffee, papyrus, and ferns. Throughout the gardens, large rustic pots provide lovely focal points, and benches offer places to rest and appreciate the beauty of the landscape.

Hollis Garden

702 E. Orange St., Lakeland FL 33801
863-834-2280
lakelandgov.net/departments/parks-recreation-and-cultural-arts

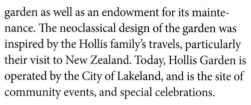

AREA: 1.2 acres

HOURS: Sept.–May: Tues.–Thurs. & Sun. 10–6, Fri. & Sat. 10–4; June–Aug.: Sun.–Sat. 10–6

ADMISSION: Free

Hollis Garden is formal display garden overlooking Lake Mirror. It is an integral part of the Lake Mirror Promenade, inspired by the City Beautiful movement that swept through the US in the late 19th and early 20th centuries. Designed by landscape architect Charles Wellford Leavitt, a student of Frederick Law Olmsted, the Promenade was completed in 1928. The original plan included a new city hall, auditorium, tennis court, shuffle board, lawn bowling and a large garden that was never built due to Florida's economic crash in 1926.

In 2000, the "long planned for" garden was finally completed due to the generosity of Lynn and Mark Hollis, a former president of Publix. The Hollis family donated the funds for the construction of the

garden as well as an endowment for its maintenance. The neoclassical design of the garden was inspired by the Hollis family's travels, particularly their visit to New Zealand. Today, Hollis Garden is operated by the City of Lakeland, and is the site of community events, and special celebrations.

Hollis Garden is divided into 16 themed garden rooms connected by labyrinthine walkways. The focal point is a neoclassical gazebo that overlooks the main axis of the garden and Lake Mirror. Stone columns and a clay barrel tile roof create a respite from the hot Florida sun. Two flanking pergolas frame lush plantings of colorful impatiens. Behind the gazebo you will find a cool, shady garden with a limestone grotto. Water drips down the grotto walls into a pool and creates a perfect environment for ferns and orchids. In front of the gazebo, the Rosette Plaza is adorned with a swan fountain. A series of bowls and runnels gently channel water from the fountain down into Lake Mirror.

The botanical display features more than 10,000 flowers, ornamental shrubs and native trees. Some are planted in color-themed rooms such as the Yellow, Red and White Rooms. Other are grouped by plant type in the Herb, Tropical, and Vegetable Rooms. A Butterfly Garden features plants dedicated to local bees, moths and butterflies. The Sustenance Orchard pays homage to Ponce de Leon, who brought citrus into the New World through Florida. Here you will find unusual trees like BlackBerry Jam Fruit and Peanut Butter Fruit in addition to more common edibles.

The Americana Room features famous trees of American history. You will find a Water Oak from Helen Keller's home, an oak from Abraham Lincoln's birthplace, a sycamore from Susan B. Anthony's grave, and a weeping willow from Elvis Presley's front yard. Plants from other parts of the world include a Frankincense tree and the Balm of Gilead.

Bonnet Springs Park

400 Bonnet Springs Blvd., Lakeland FL 33815
863-732-7000
bonnetspringspark.com

AREA: 168 acres

HOURS: Daily 6–dusk

ADMISSION: Free

AMENITIES: 👫 🏕 ❄ 🍼

EVENTS: Family, wellness, cultural, and nature programs

"Great cities have a great park" was the mantra that guided the creation of the 168-acre Bonnet Springs Park. Located just blocks from downtown Lakeland, the park tells the uplifting story of a remediation effort that transformed a former brownfield property into a green oasis.

The park was once the home of the Lakeland Railroad, a major freight hub in Central Florida that supplied the East Coast with citrus and phosphorus. Here, coal-powered locomotives were repaired, store and moved. Lakeland Railroad was the largest employer in the city until it departed in 1952, leaving behind a polluted landscape that had been slowly degraded since the 1880s. For several decades, various attempts were made to reuse the site. Finally in 2015, a group of local community advocates and philanthropists created a bold new vision for the site: a beautiful park that would benefit the community as well as the natural environment.

A multidisciplinary consulting team led by Sasaki landscape architects made the vision into reality.

Constructing the park involved removing 36 tons of garbage and remediating 300,000 cubic yards of contaminated soil that is now capped in large hills that create overlooks for the park. Wetlands and bioswales were constructed to treat over 300 acres of urban runoff. While acres of invasive exotic plants were removed, existing mature live oaks and waterways were protected and enhanced. Native Florida ecoregions, such as the Oak Hammock, Pine Flatwoods, and Baygall Swamp were carefully restored within the park. A quarter-mile-long canopy walk was built, providing a view of the magnificent 200-year-old Grandfather Oak—a centerpiece of Bonnet Springs Park. An additional 3,000 live oaks, maples, fringetrees, dogwoods, cedars, pines, magnolias, and crape myrtles were planted to create groves in the landscape. Along with the new trees, thousands of perennials, grasses, ground covers and edible plants now support the environment and create a beautiful horticultural setting.

What was once a barren brownfield site on the banks of Lake Bonnet is now a rolling landscape of natural plantings, creative playgrounds, a botanic garden, boardwalks, pedestrian and bike paths, pavilions, a tree house, and a butterfly house. The park also houses four new community buildings. Interpretive exhibits at the Welcome Center highlight the region's agricultural, industrial and cultural history. In the Nature Center you will find interactive exhibits that showcase the native plants and animals of Florida. The Events Center is surrounded by edible gardens, and the Florida Children's Museum provides two floors of science, discover and creative play. Amazingly, Bonnet Springs Park was entirely funded through private donations and brownfield redevelopment credits.

Completed in 2022, Bonnet Springs Park has become even more than it set out to be: an ecological jewel, a center for the community, and a destination for cultural experiences.

Florida Botanical Gardens

12520 Ulmerton Rd., Largo, FL 33774
727-582-2100
flbgfoundation.org

AREA: 30 acres of gardens
HOURS: Daily 7–5
ADMISSION: Free
AMENITIES: 🚻 👨‍👩‍👧 👶
EVENTS: Holiday Lights in the Gardens, Pumpkin Fest, Gift & Plant Sale

Florida Botanical Gardens showcases the flora, fauna, and native habitats of west Florida. Located in Pinellas County, the gardens are adjacent to Heritage Village, providing visitors with a single location where they can learn about both Florida's natural and cultural history.

The gardens began on a modest 10-acre site occupied by the University of Florida Extension Service. In the late 1990s, a small group of dedicated garden lovers began to pursue their dream of transforming this small site into a full-fledged botanical garden that would serve the community. Although land was available, it presented many challenges. After several years of site evaluation, design, clearing, and construction, the gardens opened to the public in late 2000.

Today, Florida Botanical Gardens is a verdant, 30-acre oasis where 10,000 plants are displayed in diverse gardens. A colorful Butterfly Garden with fluttering butterflies greets you at the Visitor Center. A bridge with a pavilion overlooking McKay Creek offers lovely views of turtles, fish, alligators, and birds. The adjoining McKay Creek Plaza is home to several themed gardens. The walled Wedding Garden is a lovely destination for weddings and other celebrations. Its four corners feature a Rose Garden, Topiary Garden, Cottage Garden, and Jazz Garden. Paths lead from this plaza to an informal Palm Garden with colorful ti plants, cycads, ferns, and crotons. The Tropical Courtyard is inspired by the walled gardens of southern Florida, with shade trees, covered porches, plant-smothered pergolas, and pots of colorful flowers. It is richly planted with

a variety of bromeliads, ti plants, and gingers. From there, the Tropical Walk follows a winding stream through beds of exotic plants from Australia, China, Japan, and the tropical islands.

The Vinery is an interesting display garden of both tropical and temperate vines such as bleeding heart vine, blue thunbergia, purple passion flower, and golden chalice vine. The Tropical Fruit Garden is popular with visitors because a wide variety of fruit trees and shrubs are beautifully displayed and labeled. You will find both edible and ornamental bananas, star fruit, avocados, mangoes, citrus, pomegranates, figs, papayas, pineapples, and more. A vivid mural adorns this garden. Other collections of note include the Cactus/Succulent Garden, plantings of camellias, an Herb Garden, and a Native Plant Garden.

Water is a major element throughout the gardens, from McKay Creek to large and small ponds, winding waterways, and whimsical fountains. The Wetlands Walkway and Wildlife Overlook allow you to visit parts of the diverse aquatic ecosystem and observe native birds and reptiles in their natu-

ral setting.

The latest addition is the Majeed Discovery Garden, a two-acre children's garden with exploratory trails, nature-themed play areas, an outdoor classroom, and educational exhibits to inspire little budding gardeners. The Music Forest, Pollinator Landing, Trunk Jump and the Bamboo Bridge are just a few of the areas that will delight children.

Eureka Springs Conservation Park

6400 Eureka Springs Rd., Tampa, FL 33610
813-744-5536
hillsboroughcounty.org/en/locations/eureka-springs

AREA: 31 acres

HOURS: Daily 8–6

ADMISSION: $2 per car

AMENITIES:

The Eureka Springs Conservation Park is a lovely stroll garden not far from the urban sprawl of Tampa. It was donated to Hillsborough County in 1967 by businessman Albert Greensburg who stipulated that it remain a public garden for the community to enjoy.

Greensburg grew up in Chicago as the son of a fish farmer. After service in the Navy during World War I, his job as a traveling salesman brought him to Florida. Florida's mild climate and abundant water made it the perfect place to cultivate fish and plants for the burgeoning aquarium industry. At that time, the industry was supplied almost entirely by fish

and plants imported from the tropics. Greensburg purchased 80 acres of land with 11 crystal-clear springs and named his property Eureka Springs. He dug ponds, built greenhouses, and started raising platies, swordtails, barbs, gouramis, tetras, and Siamese fighting fish. An amateur botanist, he traveled the world to find unusual aquatic plants such as cryptocoryne, Madagascar lace plants, and Amazon swords, which he imported and propagated in concrete tanks. Being a savvy salesman, he was able to create demand for his fish and aquarium plants in the North and as a result founded Florida's $60 million-a-year aquaculture industry.

The 31-acre plot of land that Greensburg donated to the county was filled with exotic plants that he had collected on his travels. The gardens now contain the largest public collection of ferns in the state, a rose garden, and rare bromeliads and orchids displayed in a small greenhouse. Mondo grass-edged brick paths wind through plantings of palms, cycads, and live oaks and past a slow-moving spring filled with water lilies. Beyond the garden, a 1,700-foot boardwalk takes you through a floodplain of maples, oaks, and cypresses—an ideal spot for bird watching.

USF Botanical Gardens

12210 USF Pine Dr., Tampa, FL 33612
813-974-2329
usf.edu/arts-sciences/ecore

AREA: 7 acres of gardens
HOURS: Tues.–Sun. 9–4
ADMISSION: $5
AMENITIES:
EVENTS: Plant festivals, educational workshops

University of South Florida Botanical Gardens is home to six acres of demonstration and research gardens and a ten-acre greenbelt on the west end of the large campus. Its mission is "to foster appreciation, understanding, and stewardship of our natural and cultural botanical heritage through living plant collections, displays, education, and research." This mission extends to students, faculty, and staff as well as local gardeners, homeowners, and campus visitors.

When the gardens were established in 1969, the land was little more than wilderness along a small marshy pond. During the 1970s and 1980s, the gardens served primarily as a teaching and research facility for the biology department. At that time many of the temperate, subtropical, and tropical trees were planted, and the palm garden, wetland forest, and sand scrub beds were installed. Research continues in the gardens and greenhouses and is now focused on medicinal botany and environmental engineering.

Today, the gardens are home to 3,000 plant taxa from all over the world and are a hub for local gardeners and horticultural societies as well as the campus community. The Tampa Orchid Club maintains an orchid collection that numbers in the thousands. Orchids are circulated from greenhouses to the shade garden when they come into bloom. The Bromeliad Guild and Society maintains a display garden of these colorful foliage plants that are perfect for Florida gardens. Some of the rare bromeliads in this garden take 20 years to bloom! The Central Florida Cactus and Succulent Society displays hundreds of plants that thrive in the sandy soil of Florida and require no irrigation. All of the societies actively propagate their plants, which are then sold in the plant shop.

Other collections of note include hoyas and aroids, which constitute many of the houseplants sold throughout the United States: pothos, philodendrons, monsteras, and peace lilies, to name a few. These plants have adapted to low-light conditions in their native forest-floor habitats. You will also find the Rare Fruit Council's orchard of longans, lychees, macadamias, pears, peaches, japoticabas, star fruit, avocados, and olives.

In addition to teaching gardeners about plants that will thrive in their climate, USF Botanical Gardens demonstrates how to create a healthy ecosystem. The gardens are filled with native plants that

support bees, butterflies, and migratory birds, and they feature an onsite apiary. USF hosts educational workshops, a certified bee-keeping course, and plant festivals where staff, local nurseries, and horticultural societies share expertise and sell rare and unusual plants.

Gizella Kopsick Palm Arboretum

605 11th Ave. NE, St. Petersburg, FL 33701
727-893-7441
stpeteparksrec.org/gizellakopsick

AREA: 2 acres
HOURS: Daily sunrise–11 pm
ADMISSION: Free

Located on the shore of beautiful Tampa Bay, Gizella Kopsick Palm Arboretum showcases an astounding collection of palms and cycads from all over the world. The public is able to enjoy this free arboretum thanks to the determination of a local resident, the charitable gift of a frail lady chef, and the horticultural curiosity of a gentleman surgeon and his son.

The arboretum was founded in 1976 when local resident and park volunteer Elva Rouse proposed that the two acres that had once been the city

mini-golf course be converted into an arboretum. With a generous gift of stock from Gizella Kopsick, the city purchased its first 60 palms and installed brick pathways, a gazebo, and conversation corners with wooden benches. The park was designed to meet the needs of the handicapped, which included Kopsick, who was confined to a wheelchair. The arboretum was dedicated to Kopsick on May 16, 1977, her 100th birthday.

Kopsick emigrated from Austria-Hungary to New York in the 1880s and became a chef for wealthy families. One of her employers, industrialist George Blumenthal, advised her, "Don't buy anything; invest in stock." She followed his advice, and her gift of $16,000 to the arboretum created a lasting legacy.

In 2014 the arboretum acquired an amazing collection of rare cycads from the estate of Dr. U. A. Young of South Tampa. For more than 50 years, Dr. Young, an orthopedic surgeon, traveled throughout the world, collecting rare cycad plants and seeds. His son Brad, a botanist, continued this legacy. As a student, Brad found the seeds of the endangered *Cycas scratchleyana* atop a tree in a remote village in Papua, New Guinea. When the arboretum acquired the collection of mature specimens, it was valued by the Cycad Society at $360,000. More than 100 of the rare cycads are no longer available to American botanists and nearly extinct in their native habitats.

Prehistoric cycads are the earth's original seed-bearing plants. They are considered "living fossils" and were very prevalent during the Jurassic period, some 200 million years ago, along with dinosaurs, reptiles, and the first birds. Today, only a handful of cycads species exist in the wild, and many are facing extinction. Cycads have a crown of large compound leaves and a stout trunk, and both male and female plants produce cones. Although there are about 300 recognized species of cycads, they are among the world's most threatened plant families. Common cycads in Florida are the sagos, which are

popular in home landscapes. Coontie is the only cycad native to Florida.

Strolling on the pathways of the arboretum, it is easy to appreciate the variety of size, form, texture, color, and growth habits of the palms and cycads growing there. The plants are a horticultural United Nations, representing Burma, Myanmar, Vietnam, India, Malaysia, Thailand, Sri Lanka, Indonesia, South Pacific Islands, China, Japan, Madagascar, Mozambique, Kenya, Tanzania, Brazil, and Honduras, just to name a few. Visiting an arboretum that focuses on two species of plants creates deep appreciation of the endless variety present in the natural world.

Sunken Gardens

1825 Fourth St., St. Petersburg, FL 33704
727-551-3102
sunkengardens.org

AREA: 4 acres
HOURS: Mon.–Sat. 10–4:30, Sun. noon–4:30
ADMISSION: $15
AMENITIES:

Sunken Gardens has been a landmark in St. Petersburg for almost 100 years. Winding paths lead visitors through a collection of more than 500 species of tropical plants beautifully combined in display gardens with cascading waterfalls and a flock of flamingos.

In 1903 the four-acre property was purchased by George Turner, a plumber with a passion for gardening. Turner drained a shallow lake in an ancient sinkhole to create a sunken garden, 15 feet below street level. The remaining soil was rich in micronutrients, and the sunken location provided a sheltered microclimate. This allowed Turner to grow papayas, citrus, and exotic plants from tropical regions of the world. By the 1920s Turner was operating a nursery, selling fruits and vegetables, and welcoming thousands of visitors to his beautiful gardens. In the 1950s exotic animals were added, and Sunken Gardens became one of the top ten tourist attractions in Florida. After Turner's death, the garden was operated by his sons and sold to the city of St. Petersburg in 1999.

Entering the garden, one feels transported to a tropical island. The garden provides a tranquil oasis in the midst of a bustling city. Unlike many botanical gardens, Sunken Gardens is thickly planted with more than 50,000 tropical and subtropical plants. Many of the specimens are quite large, due to their long history of protection and cultivation.

The meandering pathways wind around dramatic groupings of plants. The Palm Plaza features many varieties of palms underplanted with cycads, ti plants (cordylines), and bromeliads. One of the interesting palms that you will see is the petticoat palm, which is native to Cuba. This palm has a single gray trunk, which grows to 30 feet high. It is topped with a crown of 10 to 12 fan-shaped, stiff, erect fronds that grow in the form of a spiral. The leaves have almost no leaf stems, which gives the tree a "skirted" appearance, with the persistent older leaves forming its unique and characteristic petticoat. Another interesting palm is the triangle palm from Madagascar. Its foliage is a unique powder blue-gray, and the leaf bases form a distinctive triangle shape on the trunk. This palm creates an elegant focal point in the landscape.

As you continue throughout the garden, you will find the Coconut Grove, Bromeliad Garden, and the Butterfly Garden. The Oak Pavilion is home to majestic live oaks draped with resurrection ferns and giant monsteras. Ponds throughout the garden host brightly colored koi and a flock of beautiful flamingos. Visitors from northern climates will recognize a host of exotic houseplants and bulbs growing in drifts under the tropical trees—brightly colored crotons, snake plants, calatheas, acalyphas, cordylines, spiderworts, philodendrons and amaryllis. Look for the Eucharist lily, a type of amaryllis with star-shaped, snowy-white fragrant flowers.

There are groves of bamboos, a Desert Garden of cacti and succulents, huge bougainvillea, and a collection of hibiscus. Another exotic to look for is the black bat plant (*Tacca chantrieri*), a native of the tropical regions of Southeast Asia and China. Its bizarre black, bat-shaped flowers have long "whiskers" that can grow to 28 inches. Since the garden is so richly planted, it appears much larger than it is. You will want to return several times to study all of the plants that thrive here.

The Dalí Museum

One Dalí Blvd., St. Petersburg, FL 33701
727-823-3767
thedali.org

AREA: 4 acres
HOURS: Daily 10–6, Thurs. 10–8
ADMISSION: $29, garden is free
AMENITIES:
EVENTS: Films, cultural events

The Dalí Museum, home to more than 2,400 Salvador Dalí works, was recognized as one of the ten most interesting museums in the world by *Architectural Digest*. The museum is housed in a beautiful contemporary building built in 2011 overlooking Tampa Bay. The building itself is a work of art: a simple rectangle out of which erupts a huge geodesic glass bubble, named The Enigma, made of 1,062 triangular glass panels. The landscape surrounding the Dalí Museum incorporates elements of Dalí's homeland and of southern Florida, and illustrates Dalí's interests in duality, transformation, art, and mathematics.

The entrance to the museum is adorned with shrubs and flowers attractive to butterflies. Butterflies were particularly dear to Dalí as symbols of transformation. As you enter the museum, you cross a small bridge over a pond that collects water dripping from the immense stone that supports the corner of the building. This area is The Grotto, a shady, damp garden that is in deep contrast to the sunny, hot landscape surrounding the museum. A vertical garden or "living wall" rises from one of the pools. Colorful bromeliads contrast with the subtle greens and textures of *Epipremnum aureum* and bougainvillea. This living wall is similar in size and color to Monet's water lily paintings—an example of nature imitating art.

Large metamorphic rocks are prevalent in Dalí's paintings and create structure throughout the museum's Avant-gardens. The rocks capture the essence of Dalí's homeland—Spain's Costa Brava, or the "Fierce Coast," a rocky, windy, severe landscape just south of the Pyrenees. Other reminders of Dalí's home are the Mediterranean plants found throughout the garden—olive trees, Italian cypress, thyme, and papyrus—that provide contrast to the palms, mimosas, and ficus trees of Florida. The Wish Tree, a royal poinciana festooned with wristbands, carries the hopes and dreams of museum visitors.

Located on the South Lawn, a monumental new museum space, The Dalí Dome, houses an im-

mersive experience, Dalí Alive 360°. Visitors are invited to step into the surreal world of Dalí as art comes to life like never before in a multi-sensory art experience that envelopes visitors in 360 degrees of light and sound, illuminating the challenges and triumphs of Dalí's artistic career.

Dalí was fascinated with science and math. Look for the large pi embedded in the lawn and the golden ratio embedded in the patio under The

Enigma's Bay Vista. A 20- by- 32- foot rectangle is formed by stone pavers of varying hues. If a square section is removed, the remainder is another gold rectangle. A Fibonacci spiral is inlaid into the pavers, with a number of the Fibonacci sequence at each intersection of the spiral and the square. The Avant-garden is also adorned with Dalí's sculptures, a melting clock bench, and a fabulous pair of giant moustaches.

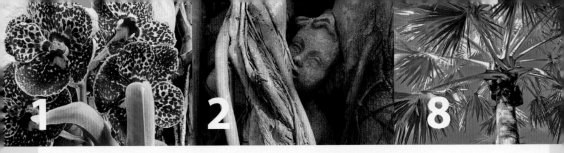

SOUTHWEST

Suggested Daily Itineraries

Sarasota Garden Club (3) or Sarasota Jungle Gardens (4)
Lunch–Bijou Garden Cafe, Sarasota
Marie Selby Botanical Gardens, Downtown Sarasota Campus, Sarasota (1)

The Ringling, Sarasota
Lunch–The Ringling

Marie Selby Botanical Gardens, Historic Spanish Point Campus, Osprey (7)
Lunch– Dockside Waterfront Grill, Venice
Monty Andrews Arboretum, Venice (8)
Garden of Five Senses, North Port (9)

Peace River Botanical & Sculpture Gardens, Punta Gorda (10)
Lunch–Harpoon Harry's, Punta Gorda

Burroughs Home and Gardens, Fort Myers (11)
Lunch–Wisteria Tea Room, Fort Myers
Sundance Orchids & Bromeliads, Fort Myers (15)

Berne Davis Gardens, Fort Myers (13)
Lunch–Pinchers, Fort Myers
Edison and Ford Winter Estates, Fort Myers (12)

Naples Botanical Gardens, Naples (18)
Lunch–Naples Botanical Garden Cafe

Naples Zoo at Caribbean Gardens, Naples (19)
Lunch–Brambles English Tea Room, Naples
Garden of Hope and Courage, Naples (20)

SOUTHWEST

Marie Selby Botanical Gardens
Downtown Sarasota Campus

1534 Mound Street, Sarasota, FL 34236
941-366-5731
selby.org

AREA: 15 acres
HOURS: Daily 10–5
ADMISSION: $28
AMENITIES:
EVENTS: Educational programs, special exhibits

Located on the shore of Sarasota Bay, Marie Selby Botanical Gardens Downton Sarasota Campus is the only botanical garden in the world dedicated to the study and conservation of epiphytes, or air plants, such as orchids, bromeliads, and gesneriads. Selby Gardens' Historic Spanish Point campus, located less than 10 miles south, showcases native Florida plants and regional history (see page 120).

Bill and Marie Selby came to Sarasota from Ohio and built a modest two-story Spanish-style house in the early 1920s. Despite their enormous wealth from oil and mining industries, the couple lived a quiet unpretentious life and became active philanthropists in the community. They both loved nature

and the outdoors and enjoyed boating, fishing, and riding. Marie was a passionate gardener. She designed the landscape around their home, and was a founding member of the Sarasota Garden Club. When she passed away in 1971, she left her property to the community as a botanical garden.

A visit to the Downtown Campus begins with a tour of the Tropical Conservatory filled with thousands of exotic, colorful plants. It takes seven on-site greenhouses to supply the conservatory with blooming specimens. These greenhouses hold the most concentrated collection of epiphytes in the world, including 6,000 orchids. You can enjoy the annual orchid show from October to December. From the conservatory, you pass through a bonsai collection, the cycad garden, and a fern garden. The Koi Pond and Waterfall is one of the loveliest spots in the garden. Shaded by surrounding trees and accented with statuary, this garden is a serene retreat.

Past the Selby House you will find an impressive stand of banyan trees that were planted in 1939 and an immense Moreton Bay fig tree with buttress roots that form a maze around its base. This grove of trees is the centerpiece of the Children's Rainforest Garden, complete with waterfall, canopy walk, rope bridge, grass huts, and a play research station.

Winding trails lead through a cactus and succulent garden, palm grove, hardwood hammock, and native plantings. A wooden boardwalk passes through

native red, white, and black mangroves, which prevent erosion of the shoreline and are critical to Florida's ecosystem. Since Selby Gardens is located on a peninsula, there are ample seating areas where you can relax and enjoy the views of the bay.

Next to the Payne Mansion, which houses the Museum of Botany and the Arts, you will find a bromeliad garden, butterfly garden, and an edible garden.

Wonderful as a public garden, Selby Gardens is even more impressive as a research institution. Since its founding, Selby Gardens botanists have participated in hundreds of expeditions to study and collect plants. Genetic properties of plants are studied in its molecular lab. Selby Gardens' Herbarium contains more than 115,000 dried specimens, and the Spirit Collection contains about 35,000 vials of orchids and gesneriads preserved in fluid. The Selby Research Library holds thousands of books, journals, prints, and digital images documenting plant systematics, evolutions, horticulture, and economic botany.

The Ringling

5401 Bay Shore Rd., Sarasota , FL 34243
941-359--5700
ringling.org

AREA: 66 acres

HOURS: Daily 10–5

ADMISSION: $25; gardens only $5

AMENITIES:

EVENTS: Garden tours Nov.–May, many events

The Ringling is a destination that features a Mediterranean Revival style mansion, a gorgeous bayfront setting with formal gardens, a fascinating circus museum, and an impressive art museum. Allow a full day to enjoy the entire site.

John Ringling was one of the five brothers who owned and operated the circus rightly called "The Greatest Show on Earth." His success with the circus and as an investor made him one of the richest men in America in the 1920s. He and his wife Mable frequented New York's exclusive auction houses and collected antique furnishings, decorations, and paintings by European Masters. Like many wealthy Americans of the time, the Ringlings made annual trips to Europe where John scouted new acts for the circus. They both fell in love with the grandeur and elegance of Venice.

In 1911 the Ringlings purchased 20 acres of waterfront property in Sarasota and began to spend their winters there. When they built their house, they wanted the design to pay homage to the Venetian Gothic mansions they encountered on their travels. The opulent 36,000- square-foot mansion was com-

pleted in 1926 and named Ca' d'Zan, or "House of John" in the dialect of their beloved Venice. During this time, John also began construction of the Museum of Art in the style of an Italian-Renaissance palazzo with 21 galleries to display his collection. John hoped that by building the museum he would make the burgeoning city of Sarasota a cultural and educational destination. The museum is now the state art museum of Florida, and in addition to the European Masters it features a collection of decorative arts, as well as Asian and contemporary art.

The Bayfront Gardens can be attributed to Mable, who was an enthusiastic gardener. When not traveling, Mable's time in Sarasota allowed her to indulge her passion for plants. The design and installation of a formal rose garden was one of Mable's larger planting projects. Completed in 1913, this 27,000-square-foot garden was laid out in a formal wagon-wheel design. Beds of roses are arranged in concentric circles around a classical *tempietto*, a temple-like structure with a decorative wrought iron dome roof. Shell paths radiate out from the tempietto like the spokes of a wagon wheel. The garden consists of 1,200 rose bushes in numerous varieties, including grandifloras, floribundas, hybrid teas, and old garden roses. European stone sculptures of courting couples enhance the setting. The entire garden is enclosed by a pergola of concrete pillars, which at one time were covered with fragrant jasmine.

North of Ca' d'Zan is the Secret Garden, a small, informal garden surrounded by a hedge and lined with shell paths. The Secret Garden features a selection native Florida species beloved by pollinators, while in Mable's day it was an eclectic selection of plants, most of which were given as gifts by visitors to the estate. It is also John and Mable's burial site.

Located between the Visitors Pavilion and the first of a series of ponds that filter water throughout the estate on its way to the Bay, is a garden with a

The beautiful Bayfront Promenade connects the Millenium Tree Trail to Ca' d'Zan.

series of sculptures surrounded by banyans and bamboo. The whimsical limestone sculptures depict entertainers in the style of the *commedia dell'arte*, a type of improvisational theater that was popular in Italy in the 16th and 17th centuries. The placement of the characters within this small garden is a nod to the Historic Asolo Theater that is located within the Visitors Pavilion.

A collection of majestic trees adorn the property, which is a Level II Arboretum. While royal palms dot the Bayfront Promenade and flank the famed statue of David in the Museum of Art's Courtyard, there are more than 30 different varieties of palms across the property. Native live oaks, South Florida slash pines, and cabbage palms can also be found on the estate. From other parts of the world are allspice trees, bo trees, bombax trees, dinnerplate trees, sausage, as well as several mesmerizingly large banyan trees.

To celebrate the year 2000, the museum added a Millenium Tree Trail on the southern edge of the property. The trail is planted with trees that are native to the region and thrive in Florida's climate.

The Museum of Art, modeled after Italian Renaissance villas that the Ringlings had visited, features a classical Renaissance-style courtyard garden. The museum is designed in a U-shape with two long loggias that connect the building to the garden and offer a shady respite. The loggias are enclosed by an ornamental balustrades and punctuated with terracotta Orci jars planted with bright purple bougainvillea. The courtyard consists of three tiered terraces linked by a central staircase. The terraces feature parterres of turf, juniper, and slash pines, accented with European sculptures in styles from the Hellenistic to Modern periods. The west end of the courtyard is home to a water feature with a moat flanked by pendant statues of reclining figures representing the Nile and Tiber Rivers.

Sarasota Jungle Gardens

3701 Bay Shore Rd., Sarasota, FL 34234
941-355-5305
sarasotajunglegardens.com

AREA: 10 acres

HOURS: Daily 10–4

ADMISSION: $24.99

AMENITIES:

EVENTS: Animal shows

Sarasota Jungle Gardens has been one of old Florida's most popular attractions for more than 80 years. Generations of families have come to admire its birds and reptiles and to wander through its lush landscape.

In the early 1930s, local newspaperman David Breed Lindsay bought 10 acres of swampy banana grove that was listed in city records as an "impenetrable swamp." Lindsay dreamed of transforming the subtropical jungle into a botanic garden. He teamed up with his friend and neighbor Pearson Conrad, who owned an adjacent nursery, and the duo created the streams and lakes on the property and laid out the gardens. They combined native species with hundreds of tropical plants imported from all over the world. Today, these prized plantings include the rare Australian nut tree, a bunya

tree, the largest Norfolk Island pine in Florida, bulrush, strangler figs, royal palms, selloums, banana trees, Peruvian apple cactus, staghorn ferns, and bald cypress. You will also find many fishtail palms, named for the unusual shape of their leaves which resemble the jagged tail of a fish. The leaves form thick, swirled layers of ruffled fronds. Fishtail palms are clustering trees that grow dense and reach heights of 20 to 25 feet.

In 1936 the somewhat manicured jungle began to attract attention from curious passersby. On New Year's Eve 1939, Sarasota Jungle Gardens officially opened to the public as a tourist attraction, charging 35 cents for adults and 10 cents for children.

As decades passed, native and exotic birds and reptiles were added to the garden. Today, more than 200 animals call the Jungle Gardens home: parrots and macaws, primates, small mammals, and dozens of snakes, lizards, iguanas, alligators, crocodiles, and other reptiles. The park's mascots are a flock of Florida's pink flamingos that freely approach you as you stroll past their pond. Jungle Gardens is the only attraction in Florida where guests are allowed to feed them by hand, which is a treat for all.

The gardens' most famous resident is a sulphur-crested white cockatoo named Frosty Sr., an octogenarian that is older than the park. Frosty was one of the original "Jail Birds"— cockatoos and parrots who were trained by California prison inmates. He came to the park in 1972. Frosty was famous for riding a scooter and pedaling a unicycle on a high wire. He appeared on *The Ed Sullivan Show* in his heyday, but retired from performing in 2018.

Most of the animals were rescued or donated to the park. Part of Jungle Gardens' mission is to educate the public about the challenges involved in caring for exotic pets. The animals provide a wonderful complement to more than a mile of paved paths

that wind around ponds and through thickets of palms and tropical plants. Plans are underway to restore the gardens and expand the exhibits.

Sarasota Garden Club

1131 Boulevard of the Arts, Sarasota, FL 34236
office@sarasotagardenclub.org
sarasotagardenclub.org

AREA: 1.3 acres

HOURS: Daily dawn–dusk

ADMISSION: Free

EVENTS: Garden tours, educational programs, flower show, music in the gardens, scholarships

The Sarasota Garden Club was founded in 1927 by a group of 26 charter members that included Mable Ringling and Marie Selby. The club's mission was to improve Sarasota's natural green spaces and to educate the public about local horticulture. Almost 100 years later, the mission remains the same, and the club has grown to more than 100 members.

In 1960 the club moved into its current home in downtown Sarasota overlooking gardens, a pond, fountain, and footbridges. The landscape is divided into nine themed garden areas designed, installed, and maintained by members. Numerous specimen

trees and shrubs provide structure, texture, and color throughout the year, including kapok, Indian hawthorn, golden rain tree, and Brazilian red cloak. Live oaks support large staghorn ferns and epiphytes. The base of one tree is surrounded by 'Moses in the Cradle' (*Tradescantia spathacea*) with its rosettes of long, waxy, striped leaves with rich purple undersides. Swaths of camellias, fiery crotons, and bromeliads create a lovely shade garden next to the building. In January, the African tulip trees are dazzling with their golden cup-shaped flowers. These trees are native to Africa's tropical rainforests and grow to become 80-foot-tall shade trees with impressive canopies. As many children in the tropics know, the blossoms of the African tulip tree are not only pretty but entertaining. Every flower bud is pressurized with a watery nectar as it expands. If you squeeze the buds just right, they make an effective water pistol with a 10 foot spray.

As you continue on the winding brick walkway, you will encounter a colorful butterfly garden maintained by the Sarasota County Butterfly Club. Since it is designed for both caterpillars and butterflies, many of the flowers need to be replanted several times a year after the caterpillars have eaten their fill. On the east side of the building is a succulent garden featuring huge blue agaves, kalanchoes and other lovely sculptural succulents.

A gravel path leads you to a lovely Japanese lantern perched on the edge of the Fountain Garden, developed by the Bay Conservancy in 2019. The restored historic fountain is the centerpiece of a large pond framed with eco-friendly shrubs, grasses, and bromeliads that form a no-mowing and no-fertilizer buffer of about 30 feet that enhances water quality. Walking paths and park benches provide areas for strolling and relaxation. The Fountain Garden is the part of The Bay Park, a 53-acre bay redevelopment project that includes conservation, recreation and cultural areas.

Sarasota Children's Garden

1670 10th Way, Sarasota, FL 34236
941-330-1711
sarasotachildrensgarden.com

AREA: 2.5 acres
HOURS: Tues.–Sun. 10–4
ADMISSION: $10 (adult)
AMENITIES:
EVENTS: Drop-in programs, summer camps

In an era when children spend so much of their time indoors with electronic entertainment, it's refreshing to find a garden that aims to change all that. Sarasota Children's Garden was founded in 2003 by Joan Marie Condon who wanted kids to discover new adventures in the natural world. Together with her husband David, artisan sons Ray and Roy, and daughter Robin, she designed an enchanted garden for creative play and for learning about the wonderful world of plants.

Past the craft and dress-up rooms, the Yellow Brick Road takes you through a tunnel of Mexican flame, chalice, and jasmine vines into the Rainforest garden of towering bamboo. The whimsical cottages of Hobbitville invite kids to play hide and seek and to prepare a meal of gourmet mud pies in the Woodland Café. The Flamingo Road leads to the gangplank of the Black Pearl pirate ship that will take you on an imaginary adventure in the lagoon. You can get lost in the Amazing Maze planted with towering Boston ferns. From there you enter into

the otherworldly Land of Od and into the Monster Garden guarded by Snuffy the Dragon. You can read Snuffy's story in a book written by Joan that is available in the shop. Snuffy is the perfect climbing structure, with his long curvy body towering above the ground. All of the metal and cement structures were sketched by Joan and built by her sons—one a welder, the other a stonemason. Look for the giant rebar spiders, the metal T-Rex, the huge purple octopus in the sand pit, and the colorful mushrooms in the Fairy Garden. The amphitheater with its stump seats provides the perfect place for bringing stories to life.

The plantings throughout the garden are used for play and for teaching. When the dombeya blooms with its bright pink pompoms, kids learn about the important role of honeybees. The red, sudsy juice of the Awapuhi shampoo ginger (*Zingiber zerumbet*) teaches kids about the use of plants in bodycare products. Through drop-in programs, children can learn about composting and insect lifecycles. The Munch, Crunch, Grow Your Lunch program teaches them about growing vegetables from seed and regrowing plants from kitchen scraps. Week-long summer camps delve deeper into growing and cooking vegetables and herbs, wilderness survival, nature crafting, herbology, and creating natural potions and lotions.

Unitarian Universalist Church of Sarasota

3975 Fruitville Rd., Sarasota, FL 34232
941-371-4974
uucsarasota.com

AREA: 2.5 acres
HOURS: Daily dawn–dusk
ADMISSION: Free

The Unitarian Universalist Church of Sarasota was founded in the 1950s. It resides on a two-and-a-half-acre campus of church buildings surrounded by gardens and mature trees. The plantings provide beauty and serenity for members as they enter the church complex and participate in services.

A mature live oak, whose crown stretches more than 30 feet in diameter, welcomes you in the parking lot. It is underplanted with shade-loving bromeliads and supports an enormous staghorn fern hanging from one of its branches. Other beds in the parking lot feature shrubs with colorful foliage and blooms. The cream and green foliage of variegated

arboricola (*Schefflera arboricola*) is enhanced by tiny red flowers and orange berries that turn black as they mature. A weeping bottlebrush tree (*Melaleuca viminalis*) provides interest with its elegant habit and whimsical flowers. It is a medium-sized tree, with graceful, pendulous branches covered in light-green leaves and large red bottlebrush flowers that add an explosion of color to the landscape.

Located in the central courtyard, the Dick and Diane Happy Memorial Garden is a serene sanctuary. Installed in 1987, this garden features hundreds of colorful bromeliads growing in the shade of a live oak and magnolia trees. Other bromeliads and orchids cling to the tree branches and trunks. A porch with teak benches and hanging orchids provides a place to rest and enjoy views of the garden.

The gardens are maintained by a talented group of volunteers who meet weekly to prune, mulch, weed, and trim. The garden crew has had to contend with interesting challenges that harm the plants, such as stray golf balls from the neighboring course and resident armadillos. The church is committed to "green" gardening practices. Plants are chosen for their drought resistance and frost hardiness. Drip irrigation is used only in the memorial garden. Rain barrels collect the runoff from summer rains and are used to water the gardens during the dry months.

Marie Selby Botanical Gardens
Historic Spanish Point Campus

337 N. Tamiami Trail, Osprey , FL 34229
941-366-5731
selby.org

AREA: 30 acres

HOURS: Daily 10-5. Boat tour of bay available

ADMISSION: $20

AMENITIES:

EVENTS: Art classes, lectures, performances

The Historic Spanish Point campus of Marie Selby Botanical Gardens is a 30-acre museum site and preserve in Osprey where visitors can explore ancient peoples, pioneer history, the Palmer legacy, and native plants. The property is a narrow point that juts out into Little Sarasota Bay, with a village of historic buildings surrounded by indigenous habitats.

Archeological records show that the site was inhabited in the Late Archaic period (4,500–3,200 years ago) by prehistoric people that had transitioned from hunters and gatherers to subsistence societies. The Archaic Midden on the site, made up of layers of shells, tools, and pottery shards, is attributed to the Calusa Native American tribe. You can walk inside to see the layers that create the midden and learn about prehistoric life.

Most of the buildings on the site are from the Pioneer Era, which began in 1867 when John Greene Webb moved his family from Utica, New York, to Florida on the advice of a Spanish trader. The Webbs named their homestead Spanish Point in his honor. They planted citrus, sugar cane, and vegetables, built a packing house to prepare their goods for market, and acquired a 10-ton schooner to transport their produce. You can enjoy an informative tour of Little Sarasota Bay on a replica of the Webbs' small boat *Magic* and see pelicans, ospreys, and local flora.

The gardens at the Historic Spanish Point Campus are from the 20th century and were built by Bertha Palmer, a wealthy Chicago woman who came to Sarasota to establish a winter estate. The queen of Gilded Age society, Palmer entertained royalty, politicians, and business magnates, collected art, and lived in lavish mansions. She purchased thousands of acres in Sarasota and became a progressive rancher, farmer, land developer, and astute businesswoman. Palmer built a 31-room mansion at Spanish Point sumptuously decorated with fine furniture, Impressionist paintings, Spode china, and family heirlooms. She employed French designers Henri and Achille Duchene to lay out the gardens and brought in thousands of exotic tropical plants. The installation required 35 master gardeners and 200 laborers.

The mansion no longer exists, but you will find

remnants of the gardens that once graced the property. A bougainvillea-covered pergola provides lovely views of the Sunken Garden with its ornamental pool and the bay beyond. The formal Duchene Lawn is bordered by two rows of queen palms and the Classic Portal, which once framed a view of Webb's Cove. A Fern Walk, entered under the Aqueduct, lies in a natural hollow created by the Archaic Midden.

The Historic Spanish Point Campus is a significant environmental site with different habitats and more than 50% of the native plant species found in the county. Nature trails and boardwalks take you through wetlands, coastal hammocks, and along a mangrove shoreline. A recently added Butterfly Garden showcases larva and nectar plants for swallowtails, monarchs, zebra longwings, and other butterflies. A new Butterfly House has also been added.

Monty Andrews Arboretum

401 Pensacola Rd., Venice, FL 34285
941-882-7433
venicegov.com

AREA: 4.5 acres

HOURS: Daily dawn–dusk

ADMISSION: Free

Whether you are new to Florida or new to gardening, the Monty Andrews Arboretum is an outdoor classroom that showcases trees and shrubs for Florida gardens. Located in a residential neighborhood in West Blalock Park, the arboretum was founded in 2006 and the city named it in 2013 to honor Lamont "Monty" Andrews for his instrumental role.

Andrews moved to Venice in 1997, and became a Master Gardener and a major supporter of local parks and beautification projects. From beach cleanups to tending city parks, Andrews donated thousands of volunteer hours on city boards and out in the field.

The arboretum encourages visitors to learn about plants while walking or relaxing. The palms and other trees are well spaced throughout the park, revealing their unique characteristics of size, form, color, bark texture, and leaf shape. The palm family consists of 2,500 species that flourish in the tropics of every continent. Palms hold plant kingdom records for the largest leaf, largest seed, and longest stem. The trunk of a mature palm, which contains many fibrous bundles of tissue in its core, can be likened to steel-reinforced concrete in its structural strength. Some palms grow in clusters, while others are solitary. They range in height from three to 100 feet. There are 12 palms that are native to Florida including the Everglades, needle, cabbage, thatch, silver, royal, buccaneer, and Miami palms, and the saw and dwarf palmettos.

The more than 100 species of trees and palms at the arboretum are labeled with information panels that provide their name, origin, mature size, drought tolerance, sunlight needs, growing tips, and general information. You will learn that Buddha belly bamboo can be propagated by dividing the rootball; that wax scraped from the leaves of caranday palm was once used to make candles; that the Bismark palm will recover from freeze damage in just one season; and that cabbage palms can be transplanted successfully. Be sure to notice the variegated mahoe tree (*Hibiscus tileaceus*), whose foliage begins as dark maroon, unfurls as pink, and finally matures to green with cream.

You will also find native shrubs, a butterfly garden, gazebos, and picnic areas. Metal animal sculptures of a Florida panther, sea turtle, tarpon, manatee, and butterfly are displayed in the park. Andrews believes that parks are a reflection of their community: "If it provides outstanding parks, it's probably an outstanding city."

Garden of the Five Senses

4299 Pan American Blvd., North Port, FL 34287
941-429-7275
northportfl.gov

AREA: 4 acres

HOURS: Daily dawn–dusk

ADMISSION: Free

The Garden of the Five Senses is a four-acre sensory garden located within a municipal park that also includes a large playground and other recreational areas. The park opened in 2007 and was dedicated to the late Jean Bruhn, a former Parks & Recreation Advisory Board member. Jean's goals were to educate town residents about the beauty and importance of the natural world and the preservation of natural resources. She envisioned a garden that would stimulate all of our natural senses: vision, hearing, touch, taste, and smell.

Wide handicapped-accessible, curved pathways lead you through the garden, with strategically placed shelters and benches for rest and relaxation. At the entrance is a large ground-level sundial. If you stand as directed, your own shadow will tell the time of day. The neighboring Fern Garden features native ferns surrounded by a ligustrum hedge. The Painer's Pallette Garden entices you with a rainbow of colors: purple crinum lily, blue plumbago, yellow lantana, red firecracker plant, and white Brazilian plume plant. The Tactile Garden invites you to touch succulent, fuzzy, and hairy leaves and rough bark. The Butterfly Garden attracts pollinators and butterflies with brightly colored, nectar-rich blooms. In contrast, the serene Zen Garden provides the sounds of trickling water and rustling bamboo. The Essence Garden provides fragrance with several varieties of jasmine, gardenias, lemongrass, and firebush.

You will also find firebush (*Hamelia patens*), a showy, vigorous shrub native to Central Florida. It grows to 15 feet in height and blooms profusely with orange and red tubular flowers from late spring through early winter. The flowers attract hummingbirds and butterflies, including the zebra longwing and Gulf fritillary. The berries are relished by songbirds and other animals. Firebush has a wide range of medicinal uses due to its antifungal and antibacterial properties.

The City of North Port planted 40 fruit trees around the Garden of the Five Senses: avocados, loquats, mangoes, peaches, Barbados cherries, and cherry guavas. These trees were planted for the residents of North Port, and the public is allowed to harvest the fruit.

Peace River Botanical & Sculpture Gardens

5827 Riverside Dr., Punta Gorda, FL 33982
941-621-8299
peacerivergardens.org

AREA: 30 acres

HOURS: Oct.–May: Tues.–Sun. 9–4;
June–Sept.: Tues.–Sun. 9–2

ADMISSION: $20

AMENITIES:

EVENTS: Gardens Aglow, special exhibits, resident artists

The Peace River Botanical & Sculpture Gardens was founded to showcase world-class sculptures and beautiful plants in a riverfront setting. It is also one of the youngest botanical gardens in the state of Florida.

The gardens are the brainchild of Roger and Linda Tetrault. The couple built a home on the Peace River in the late 1990s. As adjacent pieces of property came up for sale, the Tetraults purchased them with the intent of creating a public garden. Roger was a graduate of the United States Naval Academy and served in executive roles at General Dynamics and McDermott International. As he traveled the world for his work, he and his wife would visit art museums and gardens wherever they were. As they

collected artwork, they began to envision a public sculpture and botanical garden that would provide pleasure and inspiration for their community in Punta Gorda.

The Tetrault Family Foundation began developing the gardens in 2002. The 30-acre waterfront property encompassed five different ecosystems: marshlands, wetlands, mangroves, uplands, and a tidal basin. The gardens were designed to preserve the natural environment and mangrove marshes unique to the Peace River. Ponds were installed, walkways and boardwalks were constructed, and more than 4,500 ornamental plants and trees were planted. The Tetraults acquired and commissioned the gardens' whimsical sculptures during their international travels. They also developed an ambitious master plan for the site and provided for significant future growth. When finished, the site will be a $30-million facility and will include the Tetraults' home and extensive art collection after they pass away. Display gardens will cover 20 acres, and the remaining 10 acres will be conserved as waterways, marshland, and heritage mangroves.

The Peace River Botanical & Sculpture Gardens opened to the public in 2017. A 50-million-year-old fossil of a palm frond served as the inspiration for the gardens' logo as well as its signature massive sculpture named *Steel Palm* by Jacob Kulin (pg. 136.) The entrance to the gardens is lined with elegant royal palms and Archie Held's 9-foot-tall fountain sculpture *Fleur*. The tour begins on the south side of the gardens, where you first encounter Jack Dowd's *Yellow Andy*, a depiction of legendary pop artist Andy Warhol. Here you can view gardens devoted to hibiscus and succulents and visit a butterfly house. Colorful bougainvillea vines climb three tall metal *Tree Trellises* sculptures positioned along the pathway.

Yu Zhaoyang's *Ostriches*, a bowing couple made of aluminum and sporting bright red outfits, greets

you on the riverside portion of the site. Here a Sensory Garden entices visitors to stimulate their senses of sight, smell, touch, taste, and sound with a collection of special plants in elevated garden beds. A beautiful tiered reflecting pool is home to Carol Feuerman's hyper-realistic *New York City Slicker*, which rises out of the water with her face uplifted to catch the raindrops. Another Feuerman piece, titled *Next Summer*, floats on a silver tube, sporting a bathing suit decorated with Punta Gorda's official flower, the hibiscus. In front of the Community Center, Lin Emery's *Rondolet* oscillates in the breeze. You can join Ichwan Noor's *The Thinker* on a cube bench and contemplate the beauty of the natural pond. Plantings of architectural palms, bromeliads, stands of bamboos, and walkways lined with cathedral oak enhance the art within the gardens. A stroll on the Mangrove Marsh Boardwalk offers a close-up inspection of Florida's red, black, and white mangrove trees as well as lovely views of the river.

The gardens' vision is "to share ideals of gardening in a subtropical region, to educate our community on local flora and preservation, to share our location with local wildlife, and to inspire an artistic spirit in others by curating sculptures and fine art from around the world." It accomplishes all these goals beautifully.

Burroughs Home & Garden

2505 First St., Fort Myers, FL 33901
239-337-9505
burroughshome.com

AREA: 2.5 acres

HOURS: Tues.–Thurs. 11–1

ADMISSION: Self-guided tour $15; docent-led tour $25

AMENITIES:

EVENTS: Speaker series

Built in 1901, the Burroughs Home is credited as being the catalyst for the building boom of the early 20th century in Fort Myers. In the late 1800s, Fort Myers was a cowtown of 943 residents with no hard-surface streets, no municipal water system, no fire department, and no bank. Cattle foraged in the streets and the riverfront served as a garbage and sewage dump. Wealthy Montana cattle baron John T. Murphy was attracted to Fort Myers by advertisements claiming it to be the "Cow Capital" of the state. He fell in love with the tropical beauty of the area and purchased the riverfront lot for a winter home.

Murphy hired kit and catalogue architect George Barber to custom design the 6,000-square-foot home. When completed, the Georgian Revival masterpiece became the first showplace home in Fort

Myers, and First Street was quickly developed into "Millionaire's Row." The house was very modern for its time, with large rooms, indoor plumbing, and electricity. Large glass windows were crowned with glass sunbursts. A sweeping wraparound porch adorned the facade, and a widow's walk crowned the roof like a tiara.

After Murphy's death in 1914, the house went through several owners until it was purchased by Nelson T. Burroughs in 1920. Burroughs was an associate in the banking and cattle business in Chicago and wintered in Florida with wife, Addie, and daughters, Jettie and Mona. For the next 10 years, the home was the setting for the "most brilliant and charming entertainments of the winter season." Guests included the who's who of America, including Thomas Edison, Henry Ford, and Harvey Firestone. Upon her death in 1978, daughter Mona bequeathed the house to the city of Fort Myers, to be preserved in perpetuity as a public garden or museum.

The focal point of the landscape at the Burroughs Home is the view of the Caloosahatchee River framed by tropical palms, century-old live oaks, and a beautiful gazebo. As you gaze upon the river, the bridge to the left is the Thomas Edison Bridge, opened and dedicated to Thomas Edison on his 84th birthday in 1931. The nearby rock fountain is constructed of riprap and cobblestone and was once fed by an artesian well. The small Secret Garden was the meeting place of the Periwinkle Garden Club, whose members included Addie, Mona, and Jettie Burroughs and Mina Edison. Crinum lilies and tropical foliage plants add color under the stately trees. The front walk is lined with curving hedges and accented with potted plants.

Edison and Ford Winter Estates

2350 McGregor Blvd., Fort Myers, FL 33901
239-334-7419
edisonfordwinterestates.org

AREA: 20 acres
HOURS: Daily 9–5:30, self-guided & guided tours available
ADMISSION: $25
AMENITIES:
EVENTS: Orchid Sale and Symposium, Garden Festivals, Holiday Nights, many classes and events

The Edison and Ford Winter Estates is a wonderful place to visit for gardeners and those interested in history, science, engineering, and automobiles. These lovely homes and gardens were the former residences of master inventor Thomas Edison and automobile magnate Henry Ford. The property includes 20 acres of gardens, historic buildings, a museum, and the 1928 Edison Botanical Research Laboratory.

World-renowned inventor Thomas Edison first came to Fort Myers in 1885 in search of a warm escape from cold northern winters. He purchased more than 13 acres along the Caloosahatchee River, and shortly after he designed his plan for a winter retreat. The estate included a guest house, caretaker's cottage, laboratory, and extensive gardens. It became known as Seminole Lodge and was enjoyed by Edison, his wife Mina, and their family for six decades. The Edisons hosted many friends,

Mina and Thomas Edison

including Henry Ford, Harvey Firestone, and president-elect Herbert Hoover.

Henry Ford was a close friend of Edison since the 1890s. When he and his family visited the Edisons in Fort Myers in 1914, they also fell in love with the area. In 1916 Ford purchased the Craftsman bungalow next door and named it The Mangoes.

In 1927 Edison, Ford, and Firestone became concerned about America's dependence on foreign rubber sources for its industrial enterprises. They formed the Edison Botanic Research Corporation whose mission was to find a plant source of rubber that could be grown and produced quickly in the US. A research laboratory was built on the Edison estate and acres of plants were grown. After testing more than 17,000 plant samples, Edison eventually selected goldenrod as the most suitable.

Mina Edison, a horticulturist in her own right, loved roses as did Clara Ford. The grounds feature two rose gardens with many more rose bushes located throughout the Riverside gardens. In 1947 Mina deeded the estate to the City of Fort Myers. All of the historic structures, including the homes, gardens, and other buildings, have been restored to the 1929 time period. You will find more than 1,700 plants on the property representing 400 species from six continents. Some of the most notable include a banyan tree planted in the 1920s, allées of elegant royal palms, a collection of 100 species of palms, and more than a dozen varieties of bamboo.

Some of the bamboo is original to the grounds and was used by Edison in his light bulb experiments.

A collection of beautiful orchids greets you at the entrance to the grounds. Orchids can be seen growing on the trunks of palms throughout the gardens. Adjacent to Edison's study is the Moonlight Garden, designed in 1929 by landscape designer Ellen Biddle Shipman. Filled with night-blooming fragrant shrubs and flowers, the garden features an ornamental pool that reflects the moonlight. A tropical fruit orchard features citrus, sapote, tamarind, papaya, lychee, longan, guava, jackfruit, loquat, calamondin, and starfruit. The Edisons and Fords shared a passion for growing their own food, and the tradition continues today in the Heritage and Community Gardens.

Berne Davis Gardens

2166 Virginia Ave., Fort Myers, FL 33901
239-332-4942
fmlcgardencouncil.com

AREA: 2 acres

HOURS: Sept.–April: Tues. & Thurs. 10–1;
May–Aug.: Tues. 9–2

ADMISSION: Free

EVENTS: Flower Show, Open House

Adjacent to the Edison and Ford Winter Estates, the Berne Davis Gardens is a collection of lovely display gardens designed and maintained by the Fort Myers-Lee County Garden Council. The council is made up of 18 local garden clubs and six horticultural organizations. It hosts many educational programs on the grounds.

A handsome pergola with a large fountain greets you at the entrance to the gardens. Strolling to the right from there, winding paths lead you through display gardens of hibiscus, bonsais, and orchids planted by the horticultural societies that are members of the council. One corner is lush with hundreds of bromeliads sporting colorful foliage and exotic blooms. Another corner features a small

orchard of mangoes, star fruit, and other tropical fruits planted by the Caloosa Rare Fruit Exchange, and a small rose garden with a marble sculpture of *Loreli*, the "Siren of the Sea."

The focal point of the gardens is a lovely gazebo flanked by the rain garden with its wooden walkway. This central area of the gardens was prone to seasonal flooding, but the installation of the rain garden solved this issue. Native leather ferns and swamp lilies enjoy "wet feet." The rain garden is an excellent educational display for homeowners who face similar issues in their own gardens.

If you are visiting in late winter, be sure to see the gorgeous 10 foot-tall hedge of starburst shrub (*Cleredendrum quadirloculare*) lining the rear driveway. This shrub, which is native to New Guinea and the Philippines, displays large trusses of pale pink flowers with plum throats. It is a fast-growing shrub that reaches a height of 15 feet and displays green foliage with glossy purple undersides. Its nectar is

attractive to hummingbirds and butterflies.

The gardens were dedicated to long-time Fort Myers resident and philanthropist Berne Davis. Davis was an avid gardener and supporter of the arts, dedicated to the beautification of her community. She and her husband, Sidney, donated millions to local institutions ranging from the art center that bears their names to the Edison and Ford Winter Estates, the Uncommon Friends Foundation, and the meditation garden at a local cancer center.

Lakes Park Botanic Garden

7330 Gladiolus Dr., Fort Myers, FL 33908
239-533-7575
lakespark.org

AREA: 18 acres

HOURS: Daily dawn–dusk

ADMISSION: Free, parking fee

AMENITIES:

EVENTS: Farmers Market, Fall Festival, Storytime in the Garden, gardening classes

Lakes Park Botanic Garden is a wonderful example of landscape transformation. As late as the 1960s, this property was a man–made quarry. It was purchased by Lee County in 1978 and developed into a park with 150 acres of man-made lakes. It is a local haven for hiking, canoeing, kayaking, fishing, picnicking, bird watching, and gardening.

Hurricanes have a powerful impact on Florida gardens, and in the case of Lakes Park, the impact had a silver lining. In 2004 Hurricane Charley toppled many invasive trees throughout the park. It escalated the park's invasive removal program and an overhaul of the landscape.

The botanic garden began as a Fragrance Garden specifically designed for the visually impaired. Over the years it has grown to include a heritage rose garden, an orchard, a water garden, and a collection of succulents, tropical plants, and vines. The garden's ponds contain water lilies, reed plants, and other aquatics. Waterfalls and fountains aerate the water and help break down the organic compounds.

Cacti and succulents are showcased in a spacious strolling garden. Crested elkhorn 'White Ghost' (*Euphorbia lactea*) is a standout here. It is a striking succulent with almost white stems that lack the chlorophyll-bearing tissues necessary to produce a green coloration. The stems are covered in sharp spines and grow in a candelabra form to 10 feet in height.

The Children's Garden features a Pollination Station and Certified Butterfly Garden planted with native plants. The ABC Garden is a raised, worm-shaped bed planted with alphabetically ordered vegetables. Musical play stations shaped like flowers, lily pads, and trees add happy chimes to the garden. A Story Walk with changing children's stories guides families through the garden, and five interactive murals create fun photo ops.

The adjacent Community Garden provides a place for residents to learn to grow their own food. Experienced gardeners volunteer to teach new gardeners about all aspects of vegetable gardening, from seed starting to soil, drainage, pest control, fertilization, and other subjects that will lead to their success.

Sundance Orchids & Bromeliads

16095 S. Pebble Ln., Fort Myers, FL 33912
239-489-1234
sundanceorchids.com

HOURS: Mon.–Sat.; Oct.–May: 9–4, June–Sept.: 9–3
AMENITIES:

Sundance Orchids & Bromeliads is one of the best kept secrets in the heart of southwest Florida. Located on five acres of lush greenery, it is the largest orchid and bromeliad nursery in Fort Myers for retail and wholesale customers alike. The selection of orchids will satisfy both the collector and the casual gardener, from frilly Cattleyas, Oncidium, Encyclias, and Phalaenopsis in shades of white, yellow, pink, and purple to delicate Dendrobiums, Bulbophyllums, and Vandas imported directly from Thailand. Plants can be purchased separately

or in beautifully composed arrangements in pots or on African Mopani "living logs." In addition to orchid plants and growing supplies, Sundance offers repotting services, classes, and a "Summer Camp" for orchid owners who travel.

Bromeliads are the nursery's second focus, with a huge selection of plants available for outdoor landscaping or decoration of the lanai and indoor spaces. They come in a variety of shapes and sizes that can be displayed in creative containers, attached to trees or incorporated in landscape beds.

What truly sets Sundance apart is its commitment to simplifying orchid and bromeliad care for the customer. With a team of warm and knowledgeable staff, visitors are guided through a journey of discovery, learning the secrets of cultivating these stunning plants. Travelers can have purchases shipped to their homes or order from the nursery's website.

Like many public gardens and nurseries, Sundance Orchids grew from a hobby. Founder Lee Behrhorst retired to Florida from Pittsburgh in the 1990s. When he found that he could not create a large outdoor garden in his gated community, Lee began to collect orchids for his lanai. Hobby turned into obsession, and when his collection outgrew his house, Lee began to search for greenhouse space. In 2001 he found land with a dilapidated greenhouse that became the home for his 3,000 orchids and a small nursery business. Lee's passion evolved to include bromeliads, and as his business grew, so did the number of greenhouses. When he retired in early 2017, Lee sold the business to long-time employee and orchid enthusiast Jacki Garland and her husband Elijah Spurlin. Hurricanes Irma and Ian caused tremendous damage, but the display gardens have been replanted with 160 rare palms, trees, and shrubs to create a lovely garden destination.

PotteryScapes

27570 Old 41 Rd., Bonita Springs, FL 34135
239-947-8383
potteryscapes.com

HOURS: Mon.–Sat. 9:30—5:30, Sun. 9:30—5
AMENITIES:

From Fort Myers to Marco Island, Naples, Bonita Springs, and beyond, PotteryScapes has been adding a splash of color to Southwest Florida gardens and lanais. Their offerings include high-fired clay planters in every size, shape and color imaginable; pebble pottery, Mexican Talavera pottery, fountains, statuary, metal art, and outdoor decor, making PotteryScapes a must-see destination for gardeners in the historic Bonita Springs area.

Owners Seth and April Heyes have been in the pottery business for nearly 20 years. They bringing a vast amount of knowledge about potter to their business. Their love for travel has has inspired them to stock pottery and decorative objects from all corners of the globe.

The enormous inventory guarantees that you will find pottery to complement any style of garden, from traditional to contemporary or eclectic. A second PotteryScapes shop is located at 622 Cattlemen Road in Sarasota.

Wonder Gardens

27180 Old US 41, Bonita Springs, FL 34135
239-992-2591
wondergardens.org

AREA: 3.5 acres
HOURS: Daily 10–4
ADMISSION: $12
AMENITIES: 👥 🏛 🍼
EVENTS: Florida Landscaping Expert Certification Program

Wonder Gardens was founded by brothers Bill and Lester Piper who stumbled upon Bonita Springs during a hunting trip. In 1936 they established what was then known as The Reptile Gardens along the newly built Tamiami Trail from Tampa to Miami. They planted tropical plants native to Florida and other parts of the world. Their animal collection grew to include panthers, mountain lions, and other mammals, so the name was changed to the Everglades Wonder Gardens. For nearly 85 years this roadside attraction captured the nostalgia, history, and wonder of Old Florida.

Today, Wonder Gardens is a public-private partnership by the City of Bonita Springs and the nonprofit Bonita Wonder Gardens, Inc. It is home to more than 300 animals, many of them rescued alligators, peacocks, ducks, flamingos, parrots, macaws, fish, lizards, turtles, lorikeets, and other birds and reptiles. Some, like the many peacocks and ibises,

stroll freely through the gardens. Others are housed in beautiful green Victorian glasshouses. A small flock of flamingos (properly named a "flamboyant") enjoys a landscaped pond with a waterfall.

The animal displays as well as the botanical gardens are being updated, but the goal is to maintain the Old Florida roadside attraction vibe—kitschy and fun—but at the same time educational. The site is an old-growth jungle of palms, exotic flowers, and vegetation from all over the world. Giant kapok trees provide shade for hanging staghorn ferns and orchids. Small gardens are devoted to bromeliads, cacti and succulents, and a bonsai display. The new Native Butterfly Garden is planted with passion flowers, milkweed, and other flowers that provide food for caterpillars and nectar for butterflies. Banana trees, African mahogany trees, dombeyas, gingers, and scores of other tropicals create a lush jungle setting for the birds and animals.

Dombeya (*Dombeya burgessiae* or *wallichii*) is also called "tropical hydrangea" because of its showy, snowball-shaped flowers. Dombeyas typically bloom in January and February, and their flowers have a fragrance that is reminiscent of frosted cake. The nectar-rich flowers attract bees, birds, and butterflies.

Naples Botanical Garden

4820 Bayshore Dr., Naples, FL 34112
239-643-7275
naplesgarden.org

AREA: 170 acres

HOURS: Oct. –May: daily 9–5, June–Sept.: daily 9–2

ADMISSION: $20

AMENITIES:

EVENTS: Orchid Show, Night Lights in the Garden, Art Exhibits, and many more

The Naples Botanical Garden is a must-see destination in Southwest Florida. It is a relatively new botanical garden, having just opened to the public in 2009. Like many public gardens, it began with a vision shared by a small group of local plant enthusiasts. That vision was supported by a $5 million donation by the late Harvey Kapnick Jr. to purchase 170 acres of open space with several lakes just three miles from downtown Naples.

From its inception, the garden distinguished itself from similar institutions in key aspects. The founders set aside half the property for conservation, research, and education on native habitats. They designated the rest for a botanical paradise showcasing plants of the subtropical climate zone. World-renowned landscape architects designed the primary gardens that capture the spirit of Brazil, Southeast Asia, the Caribbean, and Southwest

Florida. These unusual international themes, as well as the cutting-edge design of the smaller gardens, create an unforgettable experience.

Entering the garden is like stepping into a painting by Post-Impressionistic Henri Rousseau. You are immediately immersed in a verdant world of exotic vegetation. Kathryn's Garden is a densely planted jungle filled with fragrance, color, and texture. From there, a winding pathway leads you to Brazil. Designed by Raymond Jungles, protégé of Burle Marx, the Kapnick Brazilian Garden reflects the famed landscape architect's visionary work. Marx introduced modernist landscape architecture to Brazil. His style was bold and architectural, inspired by Cubism, Abstractionism, and Brazilian folk art. His designs used native tropical vegetation as structural elements, large massed plantings, free-form water features, and colorful amorphous paving patterns. Marx also introduced a wide range of native Brazilian plants to the horticultural world, including nearly 50 species, cultivars, and varieties named in his honor. Many of these namesake plants are found in the garden along with significant collections of South American palms, aroids, and bromeliads. The brightly colored mosaic installation was created by the famed designer himself, and it is the only such Burle Marx piece on permanent display in the US.

The Kapnick Caribbean Garden captures the region's diverse landscape and rich cultural history. Anchored by a turquoise Caribbean bungalow surrounded by bright red bromeliads, the garden features palms, cycads, plumerias, tropical fruits, and important crops such as sugar cane, coffee, and vanilla. A long pergola is draped with blue thunbergia. The slightly elevated northern end of the garden depicts the islands' mountain regions, while the dry rocky southern point showcases cacti and succulents.

The Lea Asian Garden takes visitors along wind-

ing paths through garden "rooms" that capture the culture, spirituality, and botanical diversity of Southeast Asia. You can journey to a Javanese temple ruin and enjoy the Thai pavilion in the lotus pool. Lush plantings of bamboos, crotons, crapemyrtles, and mussaenda are adorned with Southeast Asian sculptures. The magnolia collection features many species that are threatened with extinction in the wild.

The centrally located Water Garden showcases hundreds of water lilies, cannas, and other water plants. A long boardwalk allows visitors to see the colorful blooms up close.

The smaller gardens are equally rich in plant species and design ideas. The Scott Florida Garden features a manmade waterfall, and chickee huts set among flowering trees, palms, and wildflowers. This garden sits at the property's highest point, with panoramic views in all directions. The Buehler Enabling Garden has a series of beautifully planted raised beds that allow visitors in wheelchairs to see, touch,

and smell the plants easily. The Foster Succulent Garden is a dynamic display of sculptural forms and textures for the dry garden. The Naples Garden Club Idea Garden features residentially scaled garden areas with lots of creative suggestions for the home gardener, including lush containers and succulent topiaries. The LaGrippe Orchid Garden is a gorgeous garden room with hundreds of colorful and fragrant orchids from around the globe. Grouped in pots and hanging from trees, the many different types of orchids range from dainty, leafless miniatures to plants with giant, showy blossoms that perfume the air.

The Smith Uplands Preserve displays the natural parts of the garden. You can stroll a mile-long paved path along the lakes and marshes and venture onto sandy trails to explore pine flatwoods and coastal scrub. These 90 acres of diverse habitats showcase nearly 300 species of native plants, many of them rare. They are also home to hundreds of animal species.

Naples Zoo at Caribbean Gardens

1590 Goodlette-Frank Rd., Naples, FL 34102
239-262-5409
napleszoo.org

AREA: 43 acres

HOURS: Daily 9–4:30

ADMISSION: $26.95

AMENITIES:

EVENTS: Plant sales and educational programs

Naples Zoo is a nationally accredited zoo that is housed within a historic botanical garden. You will find animals from all over the world, many of them endangered species: giraffes, Florida panthers, Malayan tiger, lemurs and orangutans among many others.

The history of Naples Zoo began with botanist Dr. Henry Nehrling. (See Nehrling Gardens) Nehrling settled in Gotha, Florida, in the 1880s, where he experimented with over 3,000 species of plants, trees, shrubs, and vines. Three hundred of those became landscape staples in Florida. When a deep freeze in 1917 killed most of his plants, Nehrling moved south to Naples, where he continued to grow, hybridize, and introduce new plants to the American public. These included caladiums, palms,

bamboos, and amaryllis. His tropical garden, now the northern section of the zoo, displayed plants from South America, Africa, Madagascar, Ceylon, the Near East, and the Far East. After Nehrling's death in 1929, the gardens went untended for years, and many of his prime specimens were lost. Julius Fleischmann, heir to the Fleischmann's Yeast and Standard Brands fortune, discovered what was left of the gardens on his first visit to Naples in 1946. After purchasing the land, he began the immense restoration of Nehrling's garden. Trails were cleared of years of accumulated debris, lakes were dug, old plantings were restored, and new species were added. By 1954 the newly named Caribbean Gardens welcomed guests once again, with spectacular gardens adorned with an array of tropical birds.

In 1967 Col. Lawrence and Nancy Jane Tetzlaff, known as Jungle Larry and Safari Jane, came to Naples in search of a warmer climate for their private collection of exotic animals. The Tetzlaffs were well-known expedition leaders, conservationists, and zoo operators in the Midwest, and they fell in love with Caribbean Gardens. After Julius Fleischmann's death, a creative merger was arranged and the property became Naples Zoo at Caribbean Gardens. Animal exhibits were carefully installed around decades-old exotic plants and trees. Some of the trees remain from the Nehrling era, while many others were added by the Fleischmans and Tetzlaffs. Notable plantings include multiple mature ficus species as well as large specimens of red sandalwood, teak tree, bunya pine, kapok tree, and cananga tree, also known as ylang-ylang. Today, the zoo continues to nurture the historic botanicals while planting new tropicals that beautifully complement the exotic wildlife.

Garden of Hope and Courage

332 8th St. North, Naples, FL 34102
239-434-6697
gardenofhopeandcourage.org

AREA: 2 acres
HOURS: Daily dawn–dusk
ADMISSION: Free
AMENITIES:

Located on the Downtown Campus of the NCH Healthcare System, the Garden of Hope and Courage serves as a peaceful oasis for patients, their families, and the doctors and nurses who care for them.

The garden is a memorial for Jan Emfield, who passed away from breast cancer in 1994, as well as all those who have been touched by this disease. Jan was diagnosed with cancer in 1990. During her treatment, she found solace in her English-style garden in Lake Minnetonka, Minnesota, and invited other cancer patients to join her there. They called her garden "the garden of hope and courage." Seeing the physical and emotional healing that her garden provided, Jan began to dream of a public garden that would do the same for others. Jan's dream became a reality when the Garden of Hope and Courage officially opened in 2004, after

14 years of planning and fundraising by lifetime friends and cofounders Richard D'Amico, Bob Emfield, Tommy Bahama, Tony Margolis, and Ludio Dalla Gasperina.

The garden's entrance is framed by two beautiful bronze feather sculptures. In the center is *Bloom*, a victorious bronze woman enveloped by a hibiscus blossom, with dedications to loved ones made by visitors at her base. The bronzes were created by local artist Kathy Spalding. As you enter the garden, your view is immediately drawn to a glimmering fountain in the center of a one-acre lake. The lake was formed in the 1980s when an artesian well was discovered during a construction project. Trustee Lester Norris convinced the board of directors to create a lake instead of filling in the site. Near the garden entrance, a shady entry garden adorned with brightly colored begonias leads to a broad curving pergola draped with pink bougainvillea. The pergola offers beautiful water views and ample seating for rest and contemplation.

A winding path encircles the lake, leading you through garden areas planted with gingers, ferns, azaleas, and annuals. Palms, magnolias, banyan trees, and live oaks provide welcome shade from the sun. Intimate seating areas are tucked along the way and sculptures adorn the path. Many of the benches are inscribed with uplifting quotes. At the far side of the lake, the Dalton Family Children's Garden surrounds a massive banyan tree hung with spherical lights. The garden is outfitted with a sandbox, wishing well, vertical chimes for music-making, a large bronze turtle, and a sculpture of children skipping over a pond. The adjacent Tommy Bahama Pavilion provides a function space for hospital patients and employees. The garden has become a therapeutic retreat for both patients and caregivers, reducing negative emotions and stress and inspiring hope and courage—the necessary weapons in the fight against cancer and all illnesses.

SOUTHEAST
Suggested Daily Itineraries

McKee Botanical Garden,
Vero Beach (1)
Lunch–McKee Botanical Garden Cafe
Heathcote Botanical Gardens,
Fort Pierce (2)

Mounts Botanical Garden, West Palm
Beach (4)
*Lunch–Paris Bakery & Cafe, West Palm
Beach*
Ann Norton Sculpture Gardens,
West Palm Beach (5)

Cluett Memorial Garden, Palm
Beach (8)
Pan's Garden, Palm Beach (6)
Lunch– Cafe Boulud, Palm Beach
The Society of the Four Arts, Palm Beach
(7)

Morikami Museum & Japanese Gardens,
Delray Beach (9)
Lunch–Morikami Museum Cafe
Butterfly World, Coconut Creek (10)

Bonnet House Museum & Gardens, Fort
Lauderdale (11)
*Lunch–Sea Watch on the Ocean, Fort
Lauderdale*
Flamingo Gardens, Davie (12)
Bamboo & Orchid Gardens, Davie (13)

The Kampong, Coconut Grove (14)
Lunch–Jaguar Restaurant, Coconut Grove
Fairchild Tropical Botanic Garden, Coral
Gables (15)

Miami Beach Botanical Garden, Miami
Beach (17)
Lunch–La Boulangerie, Key Biscane
Vizcaya, Miami (16)

SOUTHEAST

McKee Botanical Garden

350 US Highway 1, Vero Beach, FL 32962
772-794-0601
mckeegarden.org

AREA: 18 acres

HOURS: Tues.–Sat. 10–5, Sun. 12–5

ADMISSION: $20

AMENITIES:

EVENTS: Jungle Lights, Annual Motor Car Exhibition, Waterlily Celebration, and more

McKee Botanical Garden is one of Florida's oldest and most treasured natural attractions. It is home to a diverse collection of 10,000 native and tropical plants as well as one of the state's largest collections of waterlilies. Rich in history, the garden dates back to the 1930s and features two historic structures designed and built by original cofounder Waldo Sexton. More than just a destination for horticulture, McKee offers a variety of cultural and educational programs each year.

In 1922 land developers Arthur McKee and Waldo Sexton purchased the 80-acre tropical hammock with the intention of cultivating citrus. Upon touring the property, they found that its natural beauty called for a different purpose. Instead, they hired tropical landscape architect William Lyman Phillips of the Olmsted Brothers firm to design a Florida "jungle" attraction. Phillips created the design of the garden—the ponds, streams, waterfalls, trails, and vistas. He conceived the dramatic entry corridor, or pergola, to draw the attention of travelers on nearby US 1. Good friend David Fairchild sourced exotic ornamental plants, water lilies, and orchids to augment the native vegetation. When McKee Jungle

Gardens opened in 1932, it was home to an amazing plant collection as well as monkeys, elephants, lions, tigers, and alligators. By the 1940s it was one of Florida's most popular natural attractions, with more than 100,000 visitors annually.

In the 1970s attendance at the gardens waned as far bigger attractions were developed. McKee Jungle Gardens closed in 1976 and was sold to condominium developers. All but 18 acres were developed. This land lay dormant for 20 years and was about to become a shopping center when the local community banded together to save the historic landsape. With the help of The Trust for Public Land, the property was purchased and cleared by dedicated volunteers. The new McKee Botanical Garden opened in 2001, true to its founders' vision.

Today's garden appeals to visitors of all ages and abilities. There are mature banyan trees with surrealistically large root systems. The Royal Palm Grove creates a dramatic allée. The garden boasts one of the largest water lily collections in the state of Florida. There are more than 400 waterlilies of 80 night- and day-blooming varieties. The Bamboo Trail wanders through stands of towering bamboos and ends at a bamboo pavilion surrounded by a lush tropical forest. The entire landscape is a maze of winding paths, waterfalls, and ponds traversed by old stone and wooden footbridges. Don't miss the Giant Mushroom, the 2,000 year-old cypress tree, and the 35-foot- long mahogany table that hark back to the Jungle Garden days.

One of the best features is the whimsical Children's Garden, designed by landscape architect Emmanuel Didier. Here kids can "Explore, Discover, and Just Be a Kid." This fantasy world includes the Scorpion Shipwreck in the Grand Discovery Tree, a Fairy Circle and Fairy Forest Trail, Nautilus Shell Amphitheatre, Splash Garden, Water Lily Fountain, Music Maze, Bamboo Village, Blue Crab Reading Circle and Stumpery, and a Pollinator Garden.

Heathcoate Botanical Gardens

210 Savannah Rd., Fort Pierce, FL 34982
772-464-4672
heathcotebotanicalgardens.org

AREA: 5 acres
HOURS: May–Oct.: Tues.–Sat. 10–4;
Nov.–Mother's Day: Sun. 1–4
ADMISSION: $12
AMENITIES:
EVENTS: Educational programs for kids and adults

If you are interested in bonsai, be sure to visit the James J. Smith Bonsai Gallery at Heathcote Botanical Gardens, which features the largest year-round display of tropical bonsai in the country. The gallery features 128 bonsai trees, almost half of which are ficus specimens. The rest of the collection is made up of about 35 other species of plants, including dwarf jade, grape tree, bougainvillea, neea, and gumbo- limbo. Two of the most prized specimens are a 200-year-old buttonwood with a massive trunk and a twin-trunk jaboticaba, originally styled by John Naka in 1973. Many of the bonsai trees are more than 50 years old and require six people or a forklift to move them. The trees are individually

displayed on pedestals of Florida capstone in a beautifully designed Japanese strolling garden with a Bonsai Pavilion.

James J. Smith was an internationally recognized authority on bonsai and owner of a wholesale bonsai nursery in Vero Beach, Florida. He apprenticed with some of the most famous bonsai masters in the world and pioneered the use of tropical species, such as the dwarf jade tree, as bonsai. For decades Smith conducted free monthly bonsai workshops and mentored several generations of Florida bonsai artists. Smith's bonsai are displayed in important collections around the world and in numerous books. Smith donated 100 of his finest bonsai to Heathcote Botanical Gardens in 2009 when he was in his 80s. His close friend and student, Tom Kehoe, is the curator of the collection and continues Smith's work.

In addition to the Bonsai Gallery, Heathcote Botanical Gardens features an assortment of small specialty gardens including a Japanese Garden, Reflection Garden, Herb Garden, Native Plants Gardens, Butterfly Garden, Rainforest Display, and a Palm and Cycad Walk. You will find an arbor trellis covered with Dutchman's pipe in the Butterfly Garden. This vine is an important host plant for the Pipevine Swallowtail butterfly, so look for caterpillars feasting on its leaves.

Since Heathcote offers programming for children,

you will also see two unusual structures. The first is a chickee hut, built in the Seminole tradition, with open sides and a thatched roof. The second is the Pioneer House, or Florida Cracker House, a replica of the dwelling that settlers built in Florida 200 years ago. Settlers typically cooked outdoors and used the fireplace to heat the cabin. Hanging quilts created separate living and sleeping spaces inside the one-room house. The cypress wood for the Pioneer House was donated by a local volunteer. The cypress limb railing is a Native American design feature.

Port St. Lucie Botanical Gardens

2410 SE Westmoreland Blvd., Port St. Lucie, FL 34952
772-337-1959
pslbg.org

AREA: 21 acres

HOURS: Tues.–Sat. 9–5, Sun. 12–5

ADMISSION: Free, suggested donation $5

AMENITIES:

EVENTS: Botanica Garden Festival, Plant Sales, Art Show, many events

The Port St. Lucie Botanical Gardens opened in 2010 on land that was purchased by the city to protect an ecologically diverse mosaic of native plant communities. The 21-acre site is on the banks of the north fork of the St. Lucie River, with seven acres of preserved mangrove wetlands as well as ecological areas known as scrub, scrubby flatwoods, baygall, and wet flatwoods. The land had been slated for residential development. Now it is home to conservation land and 17 themed gardens enhanced with artwork, a two-acre lake with a fountain, one mile of walking paths, a pavilion for special events,

a garden center and gift shop, and many programs for the community.

The gardens are beautifully designed and offer a wide range of horticulture and design ideas. The large Butterfly Garden is lush with blooming trees, shrubs, flowers, and vines that offer food for caterpillars and nectar for mature butterflies. Passion flowers, cuphea, Dutchman's pipe, and star jasmine climb on supports, while salvia, cosmos, pentas, and lion's ear provide color and scent at ground level. A large mosaic butterfly mural creates a focal point for the garden.

The open-air Orchid Room houses over 100 rare and exotic orchids in pots that are on the ground, hung from trees, or attached to columns. The tree canopy provides a shady "roof" for the gorgeous flowers. In addition to the more common moth orchids, look for the exotic lady of the night, the vanilla orchid that produces vanilla beans, and the fragrant coconut orchid that smells like a piña colada.

Other themed gardens include the Rose Garden, whose four moon gates are smothered with purple passion flower, flame vine, sky vine, and black-eyed Susan vine; the Hibiscus Garden; the Bamboo Garden; a cool and shady Secret Garden with a gazebo; and a Palm Walk Garden. Overlooking the lake, the Bromeliad Garden offers a dazzling display of foliage color. The Native Plant Garden, maintained by a local middle school, illustrates the plants that are critical to healthy ecosystems. The Cactus and Succulent Garden shows off sculptural beauties that thrive in sandy soils without supplemental irrigation. In addition to many varieties of agave, you will find unusual sansevierias, kalanchoes, a Madagascar ocotillo, and an African milk tree. With 1,000 plants in stock, the Garden Center is a great source for plants propagated from the gardens' collections as well as decorations for the garden.

Mounts Botanical Garden

531 N. Military Trail, West Palm Beach, FL 33415
561-233-1757
mounts.org

AREA: 20 acres
HOURS: May–Oct.: Tues.–Sun. 9–3,
Nov.–April: Tues.–Sun. 10–4
ADMISSION: $10
AMENITIES:
EVENTS: Annual plant sale with vendors

Mounts Botanical Garden is named in honor of Marvin U. "Red" Mounts, Palm Beach County's first assistant agricultural agent and local hero, who tirelessly served the county for over 40 years. His territory spanned more than one million acres, and he introduced many new plants and cultivation practices to Florida farmers that improved their health as well as their income.

Red planted the Mounts' original orchard of 69 fruit trees. That first orchard has grown into a 14-acre botanical garden with 25 themed areas that continue to educate and inspire local gardeners and visitors. In addition to gardens devoted to spring bulbs and tropical foliage, you will find shade gardens, such as the Begonia Garden and the Light Tropical Shade Garden where exotic foliage is combined in stunning combinations. Look for the African sausage tree with bright red flowers, and large sausage-shaped fruits that hang down on long, rope-like stalks. In the wild, the fruits are eaten by elephants, baboons, giraffes, and hippos.

Vegetable gardeners will enjoy the beautifully planted Edible Garden and learn about growing vegetables in South Florida during the winter months. This garden is modeled after a French potager or kitchen garden. It combines both common and unusual vegetables interplanted with edible flowers and surrounded by a dooryard fruit garden. Here you will see jackfruit, snake gourds, star fruit, and bananas. A pergola planted with Philippine jade vine provides an eye-catching addition. A separate formal Herb Garden, adorned with a low bubbling fountain, displays beds of herbs grouped for cooking, medicine, and aromatherapy. Some of

the gardens illustrate how to deal with challenges on your own property. The Sun Garden of Extremes exhibits the cacti and succulents that thrive in extreme heat, harsh sunlight, low soil moisture, and low fertility. For periodic flooding, you can replicate the Dry Stream Bed or the Rain Garden with plants that tolerate rainwater runoff and filter the water before it is returned to the aquifer. The Garden of Tranquility illustrates how to incorporate Chinese, Japanese, and other Asian plants and designs to create a space for quiet meditation.

The most unique garden is the tropical wetland garden named Windows on the Floating World. A maze of open-gridded walkways placed on the surface allows you to walk through a wetland and examine the plants, fish, lizards, and wading birds that call it home. The surrounding stone walls are beautifully planted with bromeliads.

Children will enjoy the maze garden and feeding the turtles and koi in Lake Orth. They will also enjoy the Butterfly Garden, planted with milkweed, passion flowers, pentas, and panama rose with monarchs, zebra longwings, and cloudless sulphurs fluttering all around them.

Ann Norton Sculpture Gardens

253 Barcelona Rd., West Palm Beach, FL 33401
561-832-5328
ansg.org

AREA: 2 acres

HOURS: Oct.–June: Wed.–Sun. 10–4

ADMISSION: $15

AMENITIES:

EVENTS: Sculpture exhibits, musical performances

Ann Norton Sculpture Gardens features the 100-year old home, studio, and gardens of 20th-century sculptor Ann Weaver Norton. Located on the Intracoastal Waterway near downtown West Palm Beach, it is a lush oasis in the midst of the city.

Born in Selma, Alabama, Ann studied art and worked professionally in New York City. She apprenticed for five years with John Hovannes and Alexander Archipenko, who was a member of the Parisian Section d'Or with Picasso, Braque, and Gris. This group steered sculpture toward abstract, nonliteral representation. In 1943 Ann began teaching sculpture at the Norton Gallery and School of Art in West Palm Beach. It was there that she became acquainted with Ralph Norton, a major art collector and the gallery's founder. She married Norton in 1948 and moved into his home in the El Cid neighborhood of West Palm Beach. The Nortons added an art studio to the property, and Ann began sculpting full time and exhibiting her work.

In the subsequent four decades, Ann's sculpture evolved fully into abstraction. More than 100 of those works are displayed throughout the house, studio, and gardens. The gardens were designed by Ann and her friend, garden designer Sir Peter Smithers, to showcase her work. The dense plantings of 250 rare palm trees, cycads, and unusual tropicals provide a lush green backdrop for the evocative art pieces.

The gardens are divided into three sections. The first section, fronting on Barcelona Road, is the Welcome Garden. It features a large coquina patio, a grotto, and a pool with a monumental brick sculpture resembling a mountain range. This open bright

area, with its view of the Intracoastal Waterway, was used for outdoor entertaining. The lawn is framed by tall palms and tropicals that create sharp vertical walls without the customary transition of medium-sized plants. The second section is dominated by the giant figure sculpture titled *Seven Beings*. Sculpted from pink Norwegian granite, these colossal figures were inspired by sandstone formations that Ann saw in Utah. The sculpture was a memorial to her husband, who passed away just five years after they were married. This section also includes the Orchid House and Outdoor Classroom.

The third and largest section of the gardens is designed in a natural, unmanicured style and features the great brick sculptures. As you walk through the thickly planted jungle garden, you come upon seven vertical monoliths that tower to 30 feet. Built from red brick that was handmade in North Carolina, their massive form evokes the solemnity of Stonehenge. All but one are titled *Gateways* and resemble portals with evocative openings, buttresses, and arches. The dense plantings partially obscure the sculptures, adding an aura of mystery. Here the gardens are planted with native pine and mahogany in addition to palms, cycads, and tropicals. A pollinator garden provides habitat for birds, bees, and butterflies. A reflecting pool and meditation pond add to the tranquil surroundings that invite quiet contemplation.

Pan's Garden

386 Hibiscus Ave., Palm Beach, FL 33480
561-832-0731
palmbeachpreservation.org/visit/pans-garden

AREA: .5 acres

HOURS: Daily 10–4

ADMISSION: Free

Pan's Garden is Florida's first all-native botanical garden. It was established in 1994 by the Preservation Foundation of Palm Beach. The garden takes its name from the bronze statue of Pan that graces its entrance pool. The whimsical statue, designed by Frederick MacMonnies in 1890, depicts Pan, the ancient god of shepherds and wild places, playing his enchanted reed pipes. It is a fitting symbol for a garden that showcases Florida's native plants and the wildlife they support.

Pan's Garden is located on what was once a parking lot and a dilapidated house. The half-acre lot was purchased by the Preservation Foundation in 1993. With the help of the local community and a generous gift by Palm Beach resident Lydia Mann, the garden was dedicated just 18 months later. Both Mann and the foundation wanted to create a garden that was planted with disease-resistant, drought-tolerant indigenous plants to serve as an oasis for adults and children. The landscape firm of Sanchez and Maddux created a central open courtyard with a wetland area to the south and an upland area to the north. Bald cypresses, red maples, and majestic live oaks create a canopy for native shrubs, vines, wildflowers, and grasses. The garden is maintained organically, and the native plants provide food and habitats for insects, caterpillars, lizards, and birds.

The courtyard is flanked by two small Mediterranean-style buildings and pergolas. Rustic Chicago brick forms walkways through the garden. The elaborately tiled wall fountain in the central courtyard came from the historic Casa Apava estate dating back to 1918 and uses both Portugese and Mizner tiles. When Casa Apava was subdivided in 1989, the Kramer family donated sections of the estate wall to the Preservation Foundation for installation in the garden, and the wall sections were configured into the present-day fountain.

A quiet respite just blocks away from major shopping venues, Pan's Garden provides inspiration for local gardeners and educational opportunities for schoolchildren. School groups learn about natural history and how indigenous people used plants for food, medicine, and shelter.

The Society of the Four Arts

100 Four Arts Plaza, Palm Beach, FL 33480
561-655-7227
fourarts.org

AREA: 4 acres
HOURS: Daily 10–5
ADMISSION: Free, cell-phone tour available
EVENTS: Many educational and cultural events

Founded in 1936, The Society of the Four Arts is one of Palm Beach's top cultural destinations, offering art exhibits, lectures, concerts, films, and educational programs. It is also home to two libraries and two beautiful gardens—the Four Arts Botanical Gardens and the Philip Hulitar Sculpture Garden.

As you enter through the magnificent wrought iron gates, you find yourself in the botanical gardens, which were designed in 1938 to showcase the horticulture and popular gardening themes of

southern Florida. A beautiful Asian-style gate with a blue tiled roof welcomes you into the Chinese Garden and its formal square water lily pool. The surrounding garden features trees and shrubs pruned in cloud formations, bonsai specimens, and Asian statuary and lanterns accented with liriope, white orchids, and camellias. As you step into the next garden spaces, you travel through a Tropical Garden, Jungle Garden, Palm Garden, and Bromeliad Garden. The central Formal Garden is adorned with a pool and fountain flanked by sheared hedges, liriope, and roses. The Madonna Garden in the corner provides a seating area for quiet contemplation, with a marble relief of the Madonna overlooking a circular pool surrounded by white begonias. The Spanish Facade Garden features a well overflowing with succulents and vines and a bench decorated with Spanish tile. The botanical gardens are maintained by the Garden Club of Palm Beach.

The adjoining two-acre sculpture garden was designed by Palm Beach resident and prominent American couturier Philip Hulitar and opened to the public in 1980. It is home to 20 sculptures by world-renowned artists such as Augustus Saint-Gaudens, Jim Dine, and Lawrence Holofcener, whose *Allies* depicts Franklin D. Roosevelt and Winston Churchill. Both the botanical and the sculpture garden were redesigned in the mid-2000s by the firm Morgan Wheelock, Inc. New walkways, seating areas, and plantings were installed along with the elegant plaza paved in yellow and green Brazilian quartzite, the classical garden pavilion, vine-covered pergolas, reflecting pools, and fountains. The sculptures continue in the parking area, where Isamu Noguchi's dramatic *Intetra*, a huge tetrahedron, overlooks the Intracoastal Waterway.

Cluett Memorial Garden

The Church of Bethesda-by-the-Sea
141 S. County Rd., Palm Beach, FL 33480
561-655-4554, bbts.org

AREA: .3 acres
HOURS: Daily 8–dusk
ADMISSION: Free
AMENITIES: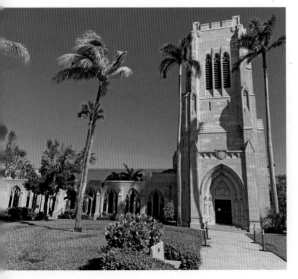

Bethesda-by-the-Sea is the oldest church in Palm Beach County. Founded in 1889, the church formerly occupied two smaller wooden buildings. Parishioners came on horseback and by boat, often traveling two or three hours to worship. The church served as the hub for charitable, social, and cultural events. As Palm Beach grew into a resort destination, Bethesda-by-the-Sea played an important part in supporting the community.

Three decades later, the congregation outgrew its facility and hired the renowned New York architectural firm Hill & Weekes to design a Gothic cathedral with a 200-foot tower. The Spanish Gothic church was modeled after the Cathedral at Leon in Spain. The cornerstone bears the years 1513, the year Ponce De Leon first landed on Florida's coastline, and 1925, the year ground was broken on the site. Secreted inside that stone is a letter from the King of Spain. Inside the church, paintings, sculptures, hand-carved wood figures, mosaics, and stained glass windows tell the story of Christianity. The adjoining rectory was designed in 1924 by Marion Sims Wyeth in a Spanish style with stucco walls, heraldic motifs, and an ornate pediment. The rectory is built around a courtyard with a central fountain adorned with Spanish tile.

The garden was commissioned in 1931 by Nellie Cluett whose parents were founding members of the church. Cluett hired Walter Thomas of Philadelphia to design a garden in their memory. The small garden is Italian in style, dominated by a central water feature and formal parterres.

Water is an important theme in this garden since the church takes its name from the healing pool of Bethesda, where, according to the Gospel of John, Jesus healed a paralyzed man. Here water originates in a round stone fountain at the far end of the Color Garden. It flows into a shallow stone rill and then continues into a long sunken pool that bisects the Color Garden. Constructed from local coral stone (coquina), the pool is home to large koi. Water from the pool flows under a small arched bridge and cascades into a raised rectangular basin in the Tea Garden below. The coquina stone bridge is decorated with obelisks and ball finials, stucco, and Spanish tile. Wide stone stairs on both ends of the bridge connect the two gardens. The upper Color Garden is enclosed by a dense stand of palms. It features parterres of cruciform-shaped, clipped boxwood and twin corner gazebos for quiet contemplation. The lower Tea Garden includes a stone-paved gathering place with stone benches and an altar for outdoor worship.

Morikami Museum & Japanese Gardens

4000 Morikami Park Rd., Delray Beach, FL 33446
561-495-0233
morikami.org

AREA: 16 acres of gardens, 200 acre park
HOURS: Tues.–Sun. 10–5
ADMISSION: $16
AMENITIES: 🏛 👫 🚻 ✕
EVENTS: Educational programs, cultural events, films, lectures and changing museum exhibitions

Morikami celebrates a century-old connection between Japan and South Florida. The museum and gardens opened in 1977 and grew over the years to their current size. Visitors will find a center for Japanese culture, situated on 16 acres of authentic Japanese gardens. The center includes a museum of Japanese art, an authentic teahouse, a shop, a café, and a myriad of cultural programs. The museum houses more than 7,000 Japanese art objects and artifacts, which are rotated in themed exhibitions. The wider 200-acre park features nature trails, pine forests, and picnic areas.

The museum and gardens commemorate a small agricultural colony of Japanese farmers named Ya-

mato that existed in the area in the 1920s. One of its remaining members, George Sukeji Morikami, donated his land to Palm Beach County in the 1970s with the condition that it become a park to preserve the memory of the colony. A permanent exhibit on the history of the Yamato Colony is displayed in the original building, named the Yamato-kan, which resembles a Japanese villa. Its central open-air courtyard is adorned with a dry garden of gravel, pebbles, and small boulders.

Morikami's gardens are named Roji-en, or Garden of the Drops of Dew, and reflect six major periods of Japanese garden design, from the 9th to the 20th century. Garden designer Hoichi Kurisu captured the character and ideas of each of these time periods and wove them seamlessly into one large garden. The Shinden Garden (c. 8th–12th centuries) illustrates gardens on the estates of Kyoto nobility. These gardens featured lakes and islands adjacent to a residential complex called a *shinden*. They were usually viewed from a boat and emphasized informality and appreciation of nature.

The Paradise Garden (c. 12th–14th centuries) is a strolling garden, inspired by Buddhist philosophy, and was designed for the samurai class. Garden paths lead to a pavilion overlooking the pond in which guests would gather to enjoy the recently imported fashion of drinking tea. In contrast, the Early Rock Garden (c. 14th century) is a Zen-in-

spired dry cascade garden resembling a tumbling waterfall. It is austere, spare, and uncompromising.

The Karesansui Late Garden (c. 15th–16th centuries) is a Zen rock garden arranged in a bed of raked gravel. This type of garden was not entered. It was meant to be viewed from an adjacent temple and designed as an aid to meditation. An antithesis of gardens designed for pleasure, this austere garden helps to clear the mind of worldly attachments. The Hiraniwa Flat Garden (c. 17th–18th centuries) is a residential rock garden that is typically bordered by plants. It includes garden ornaments such as pagodas, water basins, lanterns, and stepping stones. The Modern Romantic Garden (c. late 19th–20th centuries) illustrates Western influence with elements such as lawns, paved walkways, masses of flowers, and fountains. It is a more open and naturalistic garden than those of previous centuries.

Starting at the Wisdom Ring, these gardens encircle a lake with islands, bridges, pavilions, and waterfalls. You will also find a bonsai collection, a bamboo grove, and many quiet seating areas for contemplation.

Butterfly World

3600 W. Sample Rd., Coconut Creek, FL 33073
954-977-4400
butterflyworld.com

AREA: 3 acres

HOURS: Mon.–Sat. 9–5, Sun. 11–5

ADMISSION: $32.50, $22.50 children 3–11

AMENITIES:

Like many gardens in Florida, Butterfly World is the result of one person's hobby gone wild. Growing up on a farm in Illinois, Ronald Boender always had a fascination with butterflies. After moving to Florida in 1968, the retired engineer decided to pursue his interest by raising local butterflies at his home. The hobby turned into a business in 1984 when Boender founded a commercial butterfly farm that sold "farmed" butterflies to zoos and universities. Inspiration for Butterfly World came from Clive Farrell, founder and owner of the London Butterfly House. In 1988 Boender and Farrell opened Butterfly World, the first butterfly house in the United States.

Today, Butterfly World is the largest butterfly park in the world, with 20,000 butterflies and hundreds of exotic birds. Entering the park, you first get a glimpse of the Laboratory, home to thousands of eggs and larva in various stages of growth. Since its inception, Butterfly World has raised more than a million butterflies. From there you enter the three butterfly aviaries— the Paradise Adventure

Aviary, the Tropical Rain Forest, and the Hanging Gardens—where thousands of butterflies thrive in re-creations of their native habitats. As you walk through these indoor gardens with flowers, tropical plants, waterfalls, and classical music, you will encounter more than 80 butterfly species from Asia, South and Central America, and the Philippines. Since butterflies are short-lived, different species are introduced from week to week. Some of the favorites include the owl butterfly and the brilliant blue morpho. Be sure to look for the Piano Key butterfly, a black, white, and red hybrid with a pattern resembling piano keys all along the bottom of its hind wings. It was developed by Boender and has become his signature butterfly.

The aviaries are home to a huge floral collection that Boender amassed in his travels, with about 100 flowering orchids on display at all times. The Hanging Garden is filled with hanging baskets on one side and pupa-emerging cases on the other. In the 8,000-square-foot elliptical Tropical Rain Forest, colorful butterflies and birds fly freely in a landscape of caves, pools, waterfalls, and tropical rain showers. Most of the butterflies here are bright and luminous with iridescent reds, blues, and greens that mimic the tropical flora.

Blooms and butterflies continue outdoors with a rose garden, tropical specimen garden, and a vine maze that boasts 50 different passion flowers including the *Passiflora boenderi*, named after Boender. Free-flying tropical birds and lorikeets share three additional aviaries. The Butterfly Museum features an impressive international collection of mounted butterfly, moth, beetle, and scorpion specimens, while the adjacent Bug Zoo displays live giant beetles, exotic walking sticks, spiders, and mantids in small terrariums. The Garden Center sells host and nectar plants so that you can create your own butterfly garden at home.

Bonnet House Museum & Gardens

900 N. Birch Rd., Fort Lauderdale, FL 33304
954-563-5393
bonnethouse.org

AREA: 2 acres of gardens, 35 acres total
HOURS: Tues.–Fri. 11–3, Sat.–Sun. 11–4
ADMISSION: $25 Guided tours also available
AMENITIES: 🏛 👥 🏛 Audio tour
EVENTS: Holiday Magic, Orchid Festival

The former home of artists Frederic and Evelyn Bartlett provides a wonderful immersion in art, architecture, international folk art, and gardens. You will find an eclectic house with an art studio, courtyard garden, shell house, and gallery situated on 35 acres of Old Florida habitat.

Frederic Bartlett was born in 1874 in Chicago, the son of a prosperous businessman. The World's Columbian Exposition inspired him to pursue a career in art. He studied under James Whistler and Pierre Purvis Chavannes in Europe, attended the prestigious Royal Academy in Munich, and became a muralist and collector of Post-Impressionist art. Many of the masterpieces he collected by van Gogh, Matisse, Picasso, Cezanne, and Toulouse-Lautrec were later donated to the Art Institute of Chicago.

Frederic built Bonnet House with his second wife, poet Helen Louise Birch, in 1921, when Fort Lauderdale was a small outpost on the New River. He designed the main residence to resemble a Caribbean plantation house, with a central courtyard and a hallway with brightly painted doors, window frames, and ornate railings. Helen died in 1925, and it wasn't until Frederic's marriage to Evelyn Fortune Lilly in the 1930s that a renaissance of collecting and embellishing the house occurred. Frederic encouraged Evelyn to pursue her interest in art, and Evelyn became a painter in her own right. The creative couple transformed Bonnet House into a jewel box of color, pattern, and ornamentation, with paintings, antiques, and folk art collected abroad, mural-adorned ceilings, faux marbled floors, and walls inlaid with seashells.

The Bonnet House grounds are bordered by the Atlantic Ocean on one side and the Intracoastal Waterway on the other, one of the last examples of a native barrier island habitat in South Florida. Several different ecosystems can be found on the property including the Atlantic Ocean beachfront, sand dunes, a fresh water slough, mangrove wetlands, and a maritime forest. The land is a haven for fish and wildlife, migratory and indigenous birds, and for manatees that occasionally visit the canal.

The gardens and grounds display a blend of native and exotic flora. When you enter the property, a long allée of stately paperbark tea trees lines the drive. East of the boathouse is the fruit grove consisting of mango, sapodilla, guava, Surinam, cherry, avocado, mulberry, calabash, and citrus trees. The grove was carefully cultivated by the Bartletts and the fruits were favorite household delicacies.

The Bartletts enjoyed collecting seeds during their travels abroad and planting these exotics in their Florida garden. The Desert Garden at the front entrance of the house features yuccas, century plants, silver palms, saw palmetto, and other unusual plants from arid parts of the world. The freshwater

slough east of the house is lined with two rows of Australian pines. Gumbo-limbo trees, sabal palms, and paradise trees shade masses of wild coffee, silver palm, and coonties. The bonnet lily, a native water lily with yellow flowers and the property's namesake, still blooms in the slough.

The courtyard sports a formal garden of coquina walkways and parterres built around a central fountain. Various palms, hibiscus, gingers, and other lush tropical plants thrive in this protected space. Evelyn loved birds and animals, and the whimsical blue and yellow aviary was built by Frederic to house her macaws, monkeys, and other pets. Evelyn was also passionate about orchids, and her collection featured 3,000 plants. Blooming varieties are rotated regularly through the bright yellow Orchid Display House.

In 1983, Evelyn decided to preserve the house as a museum for future generations. Today the property is operated by Bonnet House, Inc.

Flamingo Gardens

3750 S. Flamingo Rd., Davie, FL 33330
954-473-2955
flamingogardens.org

AREA: 60 acres
HOURS: Daily 9:30–5
ADMISSION: $24; tram tour available
AMENITIES:

*"You are welcome to Flamingo [Gardens],
and are invited to spend as much time as
you desire, my only request being...that you
help us preserve this beauty spot for others."*
–Floyd L. Wray, 1939

Flamingo Gardens is an intriguing hybrid of a
botanical garden and a wildlife sanctuary. It was
founded in 1927 by Floyd and Jane Wray, who purchased 320 acres of swampland in the Everglades
to grow citrus. The Wrays were among the county's
first settlers. Their citrus orchard was christened
Flamingo Groves and grew to 2,000 acres with
more than 60 varieties of citrus fruits. Floyd built
his own 20-acre citrus laboratory, established
Broward's first packing house, and was a founding
director of the Port Everglades Authority. He also
installed a 12-acre botanical garden that served as a
test site and showcase for plants from tropical and
subtropical regions of the world.

The Wrays welcomed the public to the gardens.
They built a weekend home atop the live oak hammock in the groves where annual barbecues were
held on the vast lawn. Tours of the citrus groves and
botanical gardens as well as the fruit shipping area
were given daily. In addition to the nesting flamingos that were already on the property, peacocks,
alligators, and other wildlife were added. After
Floyd's death in 1969, a foundation was established
to preserve the core 60 acres of the property and to
create the botanical gardens and museum that are
now called Flamingo Gardens.

The garden that you visit today is home to more
than 3,000 tropical and subtropical plants and trees
as well as 200-year-old Southern live oaks. You
can enjoy a narrated tram tour of the property's
tropical rainforest, native hammock, wetlands, and
orchards. The arboretum boasts the largest single
collection of state champion trees in Florida, which
are the largest trees of their species in the state.

These include a cluster fig that is 70 feet high and 60 feet in circumference, a massive cuipo or canoe tree, and a giant ear tree. Exotic trees include a yellow saraca from Burma, a weeping bottlebrush from Australia, a flowering pandanus from the Philippines, a flame of forest from Southeast Asia, a mother of cocoa from Central America, an ice blue calathea from Brazil, and a Panama flame tree from Central America. Other collections of note include heliconias, gingers, and crotons, a large mango orchard, and a pollinator garden.

In 1990 Flamingo Gardens opened the Everglades Wildlife Sanctuary, which houses permanently injured or non-releasable animals native to Florida. You will find black bears, bobcats, Florida panthers, and river otters. The Bird of Prey Center displays golden and bald eagles and various owls. A half-acre Free-flight Aviary features five ecosystems unique to South Florida and is home to roseate spoonbills, wood storks, egrets, anhingas, herons, cormorants, pelicans, and cassowaries. Throughout the property, peacocks, white ibises, and iguanas roam free, just as they did almost 100 years ago during the Wrays' tenure.

The Kampong

4013 S. Douglas Rd., Coconut Grove, FL 33133
305-442-7169
ntbg.org/gardens/kampong/

AREA: 9 acres

HOURS: Tues.–Sat.: 9–4:30, last entry at 3:00 pm. Online reservations encouraged. Guided tours available Nov.–June.

ADMISSION: $17

AMENITIES: 👥

EVENTS: Art exhibits focused on conservation issues

Located on Biscayne Bay, The Kampong is dedicated to the conservation of tropical plants and ecosystems through discovery, scientific research, and education. It is one of five gardens and research facilities located in Florida and Hawaii that encompass the National Tropical Botanical Garden. "Kampong" translates as "village," and this complex of museums and gardens is becoming a hub for community learning where the public engages with plant science, history, and culture.

The buildings and plant collections that you find at The Kampong were founded by Dr. David Fairchild. His job at the US Department of Agriculture from 1897 to 1928 was to search the tropical regions of the world for plants that would bring economic and aesthetic value to the US. Considered the greatest plant explorer in modern history, Fairchild introduced 30,000 species and varieties into the US, including soybeans, pistachios, mangoes, nectar-

ines, dates, bamboos, sugar cane, ginger, cacao, coffee, guava, pineapple, kale, quinoa, avocados, and bananas, and economically important varieties of wheat, cotton, and rice. He also brought the Japanese cherry trees to Washington, DC.

In 1926 Fairchild and his wife, Marian Hubbard Bell, daughter of Alexander Graham Bell, built their home on Biscayne Bay. They named it The Kampong after similar compounds in Indonesia where Fairchild had lived while he collected plants. Here Fairchild planted many of the rare tropical trees and plants that he had collected in Southeast Asia and the Indo-Pacific, and continued to study them until his death in 1954.

In 1963 The Kampong was rescued from development by Kay and Edward Sweeney. Kay was an explorer and patron of botany herself and preserved the important plant collections. During her travels, she met horticulturist Larry Schokman and hired him to manage the property for nearly 35 years.

Some of the significant trees that you will see on the property were planted by the Fairchilds in the early 1900s. They include a giant royal poinciana, native to Madagascar; a banyan tree, native to Southeast Asia and related to the edible fig; a sapodilla, or chicle of chewing gum fame; and a huge baobab from the savannahs of East Africa, which now lies on its side. You will also find collections of Mayan breadnut trees, whose seeds produce nutritious baking flour; a grove of 35 mango varieties; citrus trees; and 23 cultivars of avocados.

Fairchild Tropical Botanic Garden

10901 Old Cutler Rd., Coral Gables, FL 33156
305-667-1651
fairchildgarden.org

AREA: 83 acres
HOURS: Daily 10–5
ADMISSION: $24.95
AMENITIES: 👥 🏛 ✖️ 🍼
EVENTS: Chocolate Garden, Orchid Show, plant sales, many educational programs

Opened to the public in 1938, the Fairchild Tropical Botanic Garden was established and named in honor of Dr. David Fairchild, the world-famous botanist and plant explorer (see The Kampong). Since its inception, this garden has developed one of the largest tropical plant collections in the world, beautifully displayed in a landscape designed by William Lyman Phillips. Plan to spend a full day here to see all of the horticultural displays and landscape areas.

William Lyman Phillips was a member of the Olmsted Brothers firm and had worked on the design of the Boston Common. When he relocated to Florida in 1925, Phillips became the premier landscape designer in the state for several decades. His work at Fairchild spanned 25 years. The formal areas of the garden are The Palm Glade, Amphitheater, Allée, and Overlook, with carefully orchestrated views, symmetrical plantings, and terraces. The plant col-

lections are organized by plant families, and sited in individual "garden rooms" to encourage study and appreciation of each family's diversity.

Water is an important and beautiful feature in the garden. Fairchild's 11 lakes and seven pools are home to water lilies, Victoria water platters, tropical aquatic plants, and contemporary sculptures. Stunning water features adorn the butterfly and tropical rainforest conservatories.

Adjacent to the visitor center is the Tropical Flower Garden, with a collection of trees and shrubs that provide color throughout the year. You will find many varieties of plumeria, tropical irises, firebush, Mexican cigar flower, and flowering gingers. The Hibiscus Collection displays gorgeous rare and endangered hibiscus from the Hawaiian and Indian Ocean islands. Nearby, the historic 7,000-foot-long Vine Pergola is smothered with a dazzling variety of tropical climbers such as the turquoise jade vine, white royal climber, bright orange flame vine, and pink Easter violet vine.

Palms are found throughout the garden, but the

13-acre Montgomery Palmetum is the core of Fairchild's world-renowned collection. More than 500 species are displayed in 30 individual garden plots, grouped to help botany students and visitors recognize their similarities and differences. The cycad collection also represents most of the world's 315 endangered species.

In the Tropical Rainforest Garden, a fog system creates clouds of mist for plants that need high humidity and cooler temperatures. Fairchild continues to collect rainforest plants from tropical America, Africa, Asia, Australia, and the Pacific Islands. This garden also features Fairchild's extensive and amazing orchid collection. The Tropical Plant Conservatory and Rare Plant House displays tropical plants that have extremely precise water, soil, shade, and humidity requirements, making them difficult to grow outdoors. It is also home to the rarest and most recently discovered tropical plants. The conservatory houses the double coconut palm, which produces the world's largest seed, and Mr. Stinky, the odiferous giant arum. A lovely Dale Chihuly sculpture adorns this space.

These are just some of the specialty gardens that you can explore at Fairchild. Others include the

Wings of the Tropics butterfly conservatory, Arid and Succulent Garden, Children's Garden, and Tropical Fruit Pavilion. Extensive trails lead around the lakes, through bamboo, Asian, and Caribbean gardens, and a series of native Florida habitats.

Vizcaya

3251 S. Miami Ave., Miami, FL 33129
305-250-9133
vizcaya.org

AREA: 50 acres total, 10 acres of gardens

HOURS: Wed.–Mon. 9:30–5:30

ADMISSION: $25

AMENITIES:

EVENTS: Farmer's Market, performances

Vizcaya is a stunning Gilded Age mansion surrounded by formal gardens overlooking Biscayne Bay in Coconut Grove. The gardens are notable for introducing classical Italian and French design aesthetics into a subtropical habitat and climate with tropical and exotic plants.

Born in 1859 in South Paris, Maine, James Deering was a retired millionaire and a bachelor in his early fifties when he began to build his magnificent estate in South Florida. Deering was afflicted with pernicious anemia, a condition for which doctors recommended sunshine and a warm climate. Vizcaya became the place where he hoped to restore his health. He loved sailing and boating and was greatly interested in landscaping and plant conservation. The creation of Vizcaya incorporated both hobbies and became the engrossing pastime of the last years of Deering's life.

Deering collaborated on the design of the villa with architect F. Burrall Hoffman Jr. and interior design-

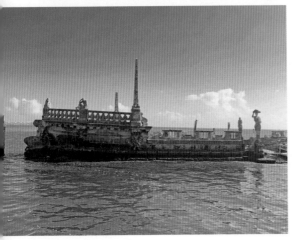

er Paul Chalfin. Deering and Chalfin spent many years traveling through Europe, collecting ideas for the Florida estate and purchasing art, antiquities, and furnishings. The duo imported gilded panels, carved mantels, and fresco ceilings from Tuscany and France to line the villa walls. Construction began in 1914, but it took years to perfect the mansion's 70-plus rooms, half of which overflow with treasures dating back to the 15th century. Inlaid marble floors, stained glass doors, silk-crowned beds, hand-painted murals, and Chinese ceramics all combine to create sumptuous interiors that rival palaces in Europe. Although historic in architectural style, the home incorporated all of the modern technology available at the time, such as a telephone switching system and a central vacuum system.

The gardens were designed by Colombian-born landscape architect Diego Suarez. Suarez adapted classical European Renaissance and Baroque landscape design to Miami's subtropical climate, terrain, and tropical plant material. The gardens were

divided into garden rooms and enclosed by ornate walls and hedges. Chalfin adorned the gardens with an abundance of architectural structures, columns and urns, elaborate fountains, and antique and commissioned sculptures. Many of the architectural elements were made of local coral stone, which is very porous and weathers quickly. To further the appearance of age, mature trees were planted in the garden, along with vines and plants that would drape themselves over the garden structures.

The gardens are connected to the house by the grand South Terrace. The terrace overlooks a large geometric parterre garden bordered by two semicircular pools. A third large pool with a central island is surrounded by low hedges whose exaggerated perspective lines dramatize the formal geometry of the gardens. The Garden Mound is the focal point of the gardens, crowned with an ornate summerhouse known as the Casino and adorned with a grand cascade and grottos. Other garden areas include the evocative Secret Garden, the intimate Theater Garden, the playful Maze Garden, the Fountain Garden, and a charming Tea House

overlooking the Bay. The formal gardens are surrounded by 25 acres of Rockland Hammock, which is the native forest in this part of Florida.

The East Terrace faces Biscayne Bay and the Barge, a breakwater built to protect the house and terrace from waves. The Barge was designed to look like a ship with fancy balustrades and statuary sculpted by American artist Alexander Stirling Calder. It was constructed of local limestone, which is very porous. The salt water and storm waves have eroded the structure and its decorative reliefs, and the rising water level has submerged the lower landing steps.

Deering's occupancy of Vizcaya began on Christmas Day 1916, with an elaborate ceremony complete with gondolas, cannons, and friends dressed in Italian peasant costumes. From then until his death in 1925, Deering spent the winter months at Vizcaya, hosting family and celebrity guests. A staff of 16 was required for the house, while an additional 26 gardeners and workers maintained

the gardens and outbuildings. Vizcaya was designed to be a self-sufficient estate to compensate for the limited commodities and services of early 1920s Miami. Some of the staff lived in the main house, while others resided in the Village—a complex of cottages, greenhouses, garages, workshops, and farm buildings that supplied fresh flowers, fruit, vegetables, milk, and eggs for the household. The Village is currently being restored to tell Vizcaya's full story and provide additional spaces for programs and community outreach.

After Deering died in 1925, Vizcaya was eventually passed down to his two nieces. The property suffered major damage from two hurricanes, which destroyed many garden statues and furnishings. In 1945 the family transferred the former Lagoon Gardens and southern grounds to the Diocese of St. Augustine and Mercy Hospital. Vizcaya opened as a public museum in 1953. Restoration work continues today to bring the mansion, gardens, and historic Village to its Gilded Age glory.

Miami Beach Botanical Garden

2000 Convention Center Dr., Miami Beach, FL 33139
305-673-7256
mbgarden.org

AREA: 3 acres

HOURS: Tues.–Sun. 9–5

ADMISSION: Free. Self-guided audio tour available

AMENITIES: 👫 👪 🚼

EVENTS: Japanese Spring Festival, art exhibits, concerts, wellness programs

The Miami Beach Botanical Garden is a quiet green oasis in the midst of the glitz and neon of South Beach. Built on the site of a golf course, the current garden was created by the Miami Beach Garden Conservancy in partnership with the City of Miami Beach in 1996. In addition to a horticultural destination, it has become a dynamic venue for cultural programs and environmental education.

An interesting way to enter the garden is via the Collins Canal Promenade, a 352-foot walkway meandering along the waterfront. Shaded by a canopy of trees and palms, the promenade is planted with wildflowers to attract pollinators. This connective pathway enables easy access to and from Miami Beach's iconic cultural sites.

Landscape architect Raymond Jungles designed the garden with the element of water as its focal point. Water reflects the sky and landscape, magnifies the space, and adds sound and motion to the garden. The central pond features a cascading oolite fountain and is home to flowering water lilies, koi, cichlids, and turtles. Red mangroves, pond apple trees, and other water lovers grow in the adjoining wetland. The water also attracts wildlife, from dragonflies and butterflies to resident cardinals, herons, hawks, and egrets. The garden is a regular stop for migratory birds such as warblers, American redstarts, and finches.

Although small in acreage, this garden is packed with interesting plants and themed garden areas. The Japanese Garden symbolizes the special relationship of Miami Beach to its sister city Fujisawa in Japan. It is built around a series of three ponds with an iconic red bridge. The ponds are surrounded by stands of tropical and sacred Bali bamboos, ferns, Japanese maples, yew pine, and a golden trumpet tree, and accented with traditional stone lanterns. The sound of water cascading over stones creates a serene Zen atmosphere.

The adjacent Native Garden is a wild area densely planted with trees and shrubs that are adapted to local soils and water conditions and support local wildlife. Featured plants include snowberry, firebush, cabbage palm, lignum vitae, live oak, and coontie.

Pinecrest Gardens

11000 Red Rd., Pinecrest, FL 33156
305-669-6990
pinecrestgardens.org

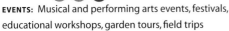

AREA: 14 acres

HOURS: Daily 9–5

ADMISSION: $5

AMENITIES:

EVENTS: Musical and performing arts events, festivals, educational workshops, garden tours, field trips

Pinecrest Gardens is a beautiful botanic garden that opened to the public in 2003 on the site of what had once been a historic Florida attraction known as Parrot Jungle.

In 1936 Franz Scherr, an Austrian immigrant and owner of a local fruit and chicken farm, dreamed of an attraction where exotic birds would "fly free." To bring his vision to life, he rented 20 acres of hammock land for a monthly fee of $25. He created a nature trail that wound through the property and left all of the native plants undisturbed. On opening day, about 100 visitors came to the garden, each paying 25 cents admission to see and hear Scherr talk about his birds, trees, and flowers. The first month's rent was made in the first day. The attraction grew to include hundreds of birds and animals and became a South Florida landmark. Among its famous visitors were Winston Churchill, Steven

Spielberg, and Jimmy Carter. In 2002 it moved to a new location and relaunched as Jungle Island.

The existing property was renamed Pinecrest Gardens and features collections of exotic and native tropical plants in a unique geologic landscape. The Lower Gardens wind through remnants of the original Snapper Creek streambed and around a series of small ponds. The streambed flows both above and below ground and includes a network of small caves and fissures. Porous limestone, which was used extensively as the gardens' building material, has been eroded by flowing water and rain into interesting rock formations with ridges, fissures, and sinkholes. One of the large sinkholes is home to colorful crabs, prawns, fish, and turtles. The Lower Gardens also include a remnant old-growth bald cypress slough. Bald cypress is an ancient tree species with rot-resistant wood and prominent cypress "knees." The slough contains a diversity of ferns and other native plants that flourish in the moisture, humidity, and shade of this environment.

The Tropical Hardwood Hammock is a transitional

area that separates the wet Lower Gardens from the dry upland areas. Large Southern live oaks, strangler figs, and gumbo-limbos create a native tree canopy that shelters a variety of exotic tropicals. Small garden rooms are tucked into the Hammock: the Hidden Garden, with its curved stone bench and circular patio; the Hammock Pavilion, with its small pond and dancing figures sculpture; and the Caribbean Garden, highlighting some of that region's flora. The largest tree in the landscape is the banyan growing in the center of the gardens. Planted more than 70 years ago, this tree would form a multi-acre grove if left unchecked.

The Dry Gardens are planted on the slopes of the Lakeview Terrace, bordering the meadow and Swan Lake. These gardens mimic the desert Southwest with shrubs, succulents, cacti, and cycads. The varying sculptural forms and foliage color of the plants creates a stunning display. Notable species in the Dry Gardens are a 125-year-old European olive (*Olea europaea*) and several large ponytail plants imported from Mexico.

Bamboo & Orchid Gardens

2325 S. Flamingo Rd., Davie, FL 33325
954-931-7733

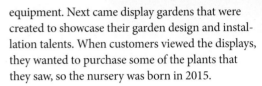

HOURS: Daily 9–5

AMENITIES:

Nestled on 2.5 acres of lush tropical landscape, Bamboo and Orchid Gardens is a charming nursery with inspirational display gardens. The business was founded by Anat and Mark Dodds in 1991 as a landscaping company dedicated to creating beautiful environments in sunny South Florida. As the landscaping company grew, the Dodds purchased a former orange grove to store their landscaping equipment. Next came display gardens that were created to showcase their garden design and installation talents. When customers viewed the displays, they wanted to purchase some of the plants that they saw, so the nursery was born in 2015.

The nursery is well stocked with plants for both indoor and outdoor gardens. As the name implies, there is a wide selection of bamboos, from 'Golden Goddess' to black bamboo, blue bamboo, and 'Alphonse Karr' that has golden canes striped with green. Orchids are Anat's special passion, and the shop carries hundreds of colorful phalaenopsis, dendrobiums, cattleyas, oncidiums, cymbidiums, and vandas.

Garden Touring Etiquette

The Society of the Four Arts, Palm Beach

Unlike public parks, gardens are designed for plant appreciation, not active recreation. Please use the following guidelines when visiting public or private gardens and nurseries:

- Smoking, fire and alcohol are generally not permitted on the premises.

- Leave pets, except service dogs, at home.

- Do not pick flowers, fruits, or plants.

- To protect the plant collections, active sports or games such as frisbee, bicycling, jogging, rollerblading, skating, ball-playing, and kites are generally not permitted in gardens.

- Do not walk in the flower beds, climb trees, or wade in ponds or water features.

- Deposit trash and recyclables in designated receptacles.

- Picnickers are usually welcome—check to see where tables are located.

- Silence your cell phones and leave radios at home. Consider your visit as an opportunity to escape from technological intrusions.

- Check in advance to see if organized gatherings and private events are permitted on the grounds.

- When photographing the garden, do not step into or place tripods in garden beds and respect the wishes of other visitors.

Eating, Shopping, and Special Interest Gardens

BEST EATERIES

Bok Tower Gardens
Cummer Museum of Art & Gardens
McKee Botanical Garden
Morikami Museum and Japanese
  Gardens
Naples Botanical Garden
The Dalí Museum
The Ringling
Walt Disney World Resort

BEST GIFT SHOPS

Bok Tower Gardens
Butterfly Rainforest
Butterfly World
Cummer Museum of Art & Gardens
The Dalí Museum
Edison and Ford Winter Estates
Fairchild Tropical Botanic Garden
Jacksonville Zoo and Gardens
Kanapaha Botanical Gardens
Morikami Museum and Japanese
  Gardens

Naples Botanical Garden
Naples Zoo at Caribbean Gardens
PotteryScapes
The Ringling
Vizcaya
Walt Disney World Resort

WHERE TO BUY PLANTS

Bamboo & Orchid Gardens
Bok Tower Gardens
Butterfly World
Edison and Ford Winter Estates
Hearthstone Gardens
Kanapaha Botanical Gardens
Lakes Park Botanic Garden
Naples Botanical Garden
Port St. Lucie Botanical Gardens
Marie Selby Botanical Gardens
Mounts Botanical Garden
Sundance Orchids & Bromeliads
USF Botanical Gardens
Washington Oaks Gardens
  State Park

AZALEA GARDENS

Alfred B. Maclay Gardens State Park
Cummer Museum of Art & Gardens
Dickson Azalea Park
Dorothy B. Oven Park
Eden Gardens State Park
Jim Houser Azalea Gardens
Kraft Azalea Gardens
Sholom Park

BUTTERFLY GARDENS

Butterfly Rainforest
Butterfly World
Fairchild Tropical Botanic Garden
Florida Botanical Gardens
Hearthstone Gardens
Kanapaha Botanical Gardens
Mounts Botanical Garden
Port St. Lucie Botanical Gardens

CAMELLIA GARDENS

Alfred B. Maclay Gardens State Park
Bok Tower Gardens

Cummer Museum of Art & Gardens
Dorothy B. Oven Park
Harry P. Leu Gardens
Wilmot Botanical Gardens

CHILDREN'S GARDENS

Bok Tower Gardens
Central Florida Zoo & Botanical
    Gardens
Jacksonville Zoo and Gardens
Flamingo Gardens
Florida Botanical Gardens
Kanapaha Botanical Gardens
Marie Selby Botanical Gardens,
    Downtown Sarasota Campus
McKee Botanical Garden
Naples Zoo at Caribbean Gardens
Sarasota Children's Garden
Sarasota Jungle Gardens
Wonder Gardens

DESERT GARDENS

Discovery Gardens
Fairchild Tropical Botanic Garden
Kanapaha Botanical Gardens
Lakes Park Botanic Garden
Mounts Botanical Garden
Pinecrest Gardens
Port St. Lucie Botanic Gardens

EDIBLE GARDENS

Bok Tower Gardens
Discovery Gardens
Edison and Ford Winter Estates
Florida Botanical Gardens
Harry P. Leu Gardens
Mounts Botanical Garden
Sarasota Children's Garden
The Kampong

ORCHID GARDENS

Bamboo & Orchid Gardens
Bonnet House Museum & Gardens

Edison and Ford Winter Estates
Fairchild Tropical Botanic Garden
Marie Selby Botanical Gardens,
    Downtown Sarasota Campus
Naples Botanical Garden
Port St. Lucie Botanical Gardens
Sundance Orchids & Bromeliads
Vizcaya

ROSE GARDENS

Central Park Rose Garden
Discovery Gardens
Edison and Ford Winter Estates
Florida Botanical Gardens
Harry P. Leu Gardens
Hearthstone Gardens
Kanapaha Botanical Gardens
Lakes Park Botanic Garden
Port St. Lucie Botanical Gardens
The Ringling
Washington Oaks Gardens State Park

GARDENS WITH ART

Albin Polasek Museum & Sculpture
    Gardens
Ann Norton Sculpture Gardens
Bonnet House Museum & Gardens
Cummer Museum of Art & Gardens
Lightner Museum
Morikami Museum and Japanese
    Gardens
Peace River Botanical & Sculpture
    Gardens
The Dalí Museum
The Ringling
The Society of the Four Arts
Vizcaya

HISTORIC HOMES TO TOUR

Albin Polasek Museum & Sculpture
    Gardens
Bok Tower Gardens/El Retiro
Bonnet House Museum & Gardens

Burroughs Home & Garden
Eden Gardens State Park
Edison and Ford Winter Estates
Flagler College
Goodwood Museum & Gardens
Harry P. Leu Gardens
Lightner Museum
Marie Selby Botanical Gardens,
    Historic Spanish Point Campus
The Casements/Rockefeller Gardens
The Ringling
Vizcaya

ARBORETUMS

Ann Norton Sculpture Gardens
Bok Tower Gardens
Central Florida Zoo & Botanical
    Gardens
Edison and Ford Winter Estates
Fairchild Tropical Botanic Garden
Flamingo Gardens
Florida Botanical Gardens
Gizella Kopsick Palm Arboretum
Jacksonville Arboretum & Gardens
Kanapaha Botanical Gardens
Marie Selby Botanical Gardens
McKee Botanical Garden
Miami Beach Botanical Garden
Monty Andrews Arboretum
Morikami Museum and Japanese
    Gardens
Mounts Botanical Garden
Naples Botanical Garden
Naples Zoo at Caribbean Gardens
Peace River Botanical & Sculpture
    Gardens
Pinecrest Gardens
Port St. Lucie Botanical Gardens
Sunken Gardens
The Kampong
The Ringling
USF Botanical Gardens
Washington Oaks Gardens State Park

Gardening Organizations & Events

PRESERVATION ORGANIZATIONS

Florida Trust for Historic Preservation
floridatrust.org

Preservation Foundation of Palm Beach
palmbeachpreservation.org

HORTICULTURAL SOCIETIES

American Bamboo Society, Florida Caribbean Chapter
bamboo.org

American Camellia Society, Atlantic Chapter
americancamellias.com

American Horticultural Society
ahsgardening.org

American Orchid Society (AOS) Florida
www.aos.org

American Rose Society, Florida Chapters
rose.org

Bonsai Society
bonsai-bsf.com

Bromeliad Society of South Florida
bssf-miami.org

Florida State Horticultural Society
fshs.org

Florida Native Plant Society
fnps.org

International Aroid Society
aroid.org

Rare Fruit Council International, Miami
rarefruitcouncil.org

South Florida Palm Society
southfloridapalmsociety.org

Tropical Fern and Exotic Plant Society
tfeps.org

Tropical Flowering Tree Society
tfts.org

GARDEN CLUB FEDERATIONS

Florida Federation of Garden Clubs, Inc.
ffgc.org

National Garden Clubs, Inc.
gardenclub.org

FLOWER AND GARDEN SHOWS

Epcot International Flower & Garden Festival
March–May, disneyworld/disneygo.com

Naples Flower Show
March, naplesgarden.org

Flower & Garden Expo
March, gardenclubofstaugustine.org

International Orchid & Bromeliad Show
April, flamingogardens.org

Orchid Garden
fairchildgarden.org

Marie Selby Botanical Gardens Orchid Show
selby.org

Resources

Mounts Botanical Garden, West Palm Beach

Bonnet House: The Life & Gift
Jayne Thomas Rice

Last Train to Paradise
Les Standiford

Edison
Edmund Morris

Florida Month-by-Month Gardening
Tom MacCubbin

Tropical & Garden Flower Identification
Graeme Teague

Nehrling's Plants, People, and Places in Early Florida
Robert W. Read

A Legacy in Bloom: Celebrating a Century of Gardens at the Cummer
Judith B. Tankard

Native Florida Plants
Robert G. Haelhle & Joan Brookwell

Guide to Historic Artists' Homes & Studios
Valerie A. Balint

Fairchild Visitor Guide
Fairchild Tropical Botanic Garden

The Botanical Gardens of Southern Florida Through Time
Ann Marie O'Phelan

The World as Garden: The Life and Writings of David Fairchild
David Lee, editor

Mr. Flagler's St. Augustine
Thomas Graham

Summer of the Dragon
Don Goodman

Photo credits

All photography except historic photos by Jana Milbocker and as noted. Jacksonville Arboretum & Botanical Gardens: 16. Wilmot Botanical Gardens: 29 center. Sholom Park: 34 bottom. Hearthstone Gardens: 36-37. Ormond Memorial Gardens: 55 bottom. Luke Milbocker: 71. The Dalí Museum: 108. The Ringling: 109. Sarasota Garden Club: 122, 123 bottom. Lakes Park Botanic Garden: 145 bottom. Sundance Orchids & Bromeliads: 146 PotteryScapes: 147 Heathcoate Botanical Gardens: 162, 163 top. Mounts Botanical Garden: 167 bottom. Morikami Museum & Japanese Gardens: 176 Bottom, 177 top. Naples Botanic Garden: 200.

Garden Index